# Beyond the Bead

# Beyond the Bead

## Making Jewelry with Unexpected Finds

Margot Potter

**NORTH LIGHT BOOKS**

Cincinnati, Ohio

**www.mycraftivity.com**

13 12 11 10 09 5 4 3 2 1

Distributed in Canada by Fraser Direct
100 Armstrong Avenue
Georgetown, ON, Canada L7G 5S4
Tel: (905) 877-4411

Distributed in the U.K. and Europe by David & Charles
Brunel House, Newton Abbot, Devon, TQ12 4PU, England
Tel: (+44) 1626 323200, Fax: (+44) 1626 323319
E-mail: postmaster@davidandcharles.co.uk

Distributed in Australia by Capricorn Link
P.O. Box 704, S. Windsor, NSW 2756 Australia
Tel: (02) 4577-3555

Library of Congress Cataloging-in-Publication Data

Potter, Margot.
  Beyond the bead : making jewelry with unexpected finds / by Margot Potter.
      p. cm.
  Includes index.
  ISBN-13: 978-1-60061-105-6
  1.  Jewelry making.  I. Title.
  TT212.P66 2009
  745.594'2--dc22
                                        2008031908

Editor: Jessica Gordon

Designer: Corrie Schaffeld

Production Coordinator: Greg Nock

Photographers: Richard Deliantoni and Christine Polomsky

Stylist: Jan Nickum

F+W PUBLICATIONS, INC.

www.fwpublications.com

# And Now for a Short Fairy Tale

Once upon a time I met a beautiful fairy godmother named Robin Beam. She showed me her magical inks and powders and potions and taught me how to make beautiful things from them. She encouraged me to use these things to make my jewelry, and I was instantly enchanted. I cannot thank her enough for opening up her toy box and inviting me to play and for introducing me to a whole new world of creative wonder. This book is dedicated to the fantabulous Robin Beam, an amazing artist and a treasured friend. It's also dedicated to my daughter, Avalon, my most intriguing creation, a magical mix of a fairy and an elf we call our little felfling. She inspires me every day to be a better human being.

## Metric Conversion Chart

| to convert | to | multiply by |
|---|---|---|
| Inches | Centimeters | 2.54 |
| Centimeters | Inches | 0.4 |
| Feet | Centimeters | 30.5 |
| Centimeters | Feet | 0.03 |
| Yards | Meters | 0.9 |
| Meters | Yards | 1.1 |
| Sq. Inches | Sq. Centimeters | 6.45 |
| Sq. Centimeters | Sq. Inches | 0.16 |
| Sq. Feet | Sq. Meters | 0.09 |
| Sq. Meters | Sq. Feet | 10.8 |
| Sq. Yards | Sq. Meters | 0.8 |
| Sq. Meters | Sq. Yards | 1.2 |
| Pounds | Kilograms | 0.45 |
| Kilograms | Pounds | 2.2 |
| Ounces | Grams | 28.3 |
| Grams | Ounces | 0.035 |

*Photo collage by Margot Potter*

## All About Margot

Much like a crow, Margot is endlessly fascinated by shiny things. She takes them back to her nest and admires them. Then she mixes them with other shiny and not-so-shiny things to make jewelry and art. She gets to play for a living, and that's a pretty darn swell gig. She's an artist, designer, author, TV personality, blogger, vocalist, actress, consultant, teacher, work-from-home mom and Jill-of-all-trades Renaissance woman. Depends on which day you ask her. Margot believes in paying it forward, random kindness and the infinite beauty of imperfection. She believes that the glass is always full, which is why she has no trouble drinking it down to the very last drop and trusting it will be filled again and again and again.

Margot spends her days in her little Amish schoolhouse in search of inspiration and joy. She is the author of The Impatient Beader series of jewelry books and coauthor of *Bead and Wire Jewelry Exposed*. She writes books to pay for her shoe addiction.

Explore more of Margot's world at her whimsical Web site: www.margotpotter.com.

## Showing the Gratitude Attitude

To my husband, Drew, for everything you do to make me feel loved and supported and to keep me sane, I love you.

Many thanks to Ranger Industries, Robin Beam and Tim Holtz for the inky good stuff.

Thank you to Rebecca Peck for being my official Emergency Ink Doctor, for that *Vogue* pattern magazine I can't stop using and for being the kind of friend every girl should have!

To the crew at Beadalon, I say verily unto you, a finer group of people never the world did see.

To Diane at Beacon, you are a peach!

To Homer of HHH, I'm so glad to have met you, and I love your products!

To Chris at Walnut Hollow, thank you so much for such fabulous tools!

Shout out to Crafty Chica for the pep talks on the phone and via e-mail; you are a true-blue friend.

High fives to Jean Yates for being there when I needed you.

To Jessica Gordon, I declare I hope we get to keep making books together foreverandaday.

To Christine Polomsky, I say you're da bestest!

To the photo crew and the design team at F+W, I say thank you for making this book look fantastic!

Thanks to Greg Hatfield for always making me feel like a Crafty Rock Star.

To the F+W sales team, thank you for getting my books out there into creative hands.

To Christine Doyle and Tonia Davenport, thank you for supporting me and my big ideas.

Finally, I want to say a hearty huzzah for my blog readers who've cheered me on through this entire process—I love you guys!

# Contents

# Introduction

Creative types tend to be extremists. Either they zero in on one art form with an unrelenting focus or they endlessly seek new materials and techniques to add to their repertoire. I am the second type of creative force. I can't do the same thing again and again and again, or I get bored senseless. I like variety and spice. I like a dash of this, a smidgen of that and a sprinkle of the other. I call it the Pu Pu Platter approach to creativity… take one from column a, one from column b and add the chef's surprise.

I have an insatiable appetite for new forms of expression that drives me to search for inspiration everywhere I go and to look for new materials and new ways of using old materials. I am relentlessly driven to learn, and when it's necessary, I invent new techniques and approaches to my work. I charge in without fear and make glorious messes and spectacular mistakes. Some of my best ideas come from screwing something up royally and finding the small seed of something brilliant underneath. My insatiable curiosity leads me to push the boundaries. It drives me to wander aimlessly through the hardware stores and the yarn aisles and the scrapbook shops and antique malls and thrift stores and wooded pathways in search of that elusive something that will jump-start a cool, new idea.

If you are a restlessly creative do-it-yourself type, you've found your book. You'll find a sampling of all kinds of techniques inside this book. If you've been using premade jewelry parts, maybe it's time to try making your own. If you're a mixed-media artist, perhaps you'd like to make some wearable pieces. And if you've been scrapbooking, why not use some of those scrapbook items to make some swanky jewelry? I know and you know there are these kooky ideas that defy any traditional approaches rolling around inside your noggin. You can search and search the world over for the perfect beads or bits to fit your vision, or you can take the bull by the proverbial horns and make your own. Why the heck not? What have you got to lose, really? Sanity is highly overrated. Neatness might count in some places, but in art studios we like to get our hands dirty.

I find the more I expand out from the center, the more I discover about myself and the richer and more nuanced my work becomes. There is so much to explore and learn that I find myself wishing for more hands and more hours in every day. Think of this book as a series of pathways down which you might wander. You may wish to travel deep into the wilderness with your trusty pith helmet and scythe, or you may wish to take a short excursion and move on to explore something else. Follow your intuition and see where it leads. Take these techniques and use them to make uniquely fascinating jewelry that reflects uniquely fascinating you. The only thing I recommend is that you enjoy yourself. So if it isn't fun, turn tail and find something that is!

Creatively yours,

*Margot*

# Building Blocks

There is an endless array of supplies out there just waiting to be transformed into beads and pendants. Here's an overview of some of the materials featured in this book. Don't stop here, though: Head out into the brave new world in an endless search for new and uncharted materials. When you incorporate unexpected finds into your jewelry, your work will always be interesting.

**① Beady Delights**

There are literally millions of bead styles—it would take an epic tome to list them all here. In the finished pieces featured in the book, I've used everything from Czech glass, Swarovski crystal and gemstones to vintage plastic, base and precious metal, and even some things that aren't really beads at all. You can find beads online, but for me, a hands-on experience is far more rewarding. Check out your local bead shops, bead shows, craft stores, antique malls, flea markets and yard sales to find beads of all sorts. Turn on your beady radar to see the potential in items other people might toss aside.

**② Inky Things**

Inks infuse your designs with color and textural interest. Different kinds of inks create different effects. Dye-based inks work differently than archival and alcohol inks. Experiment with different kinds of ink before diving into a project, including learning how inks react with any laminates and sealers you plan to use. Embossing powders give your work dimension and range from very fine to quite thick. UTEE (Ultra Thick Embossing Enamel) is a powder you can mold into pendants and beads. Once you start buying rubber stamps to use with ink pads and embossing powder, you may find yourself quickly addicted. I'm starting to believe a girl can never have too many stamps, rather like shoes.

**③ Sticky Stuff**

I have a glue drawer in my studio that is standing room only these days. I love glues, polymers, epoxies, resins, glazes and cements. You will, too—and you'll find there is always room for a new one in your arsenal.

### Glues

Different glues are suitable for different purposes. Read the labels. Each glue has a purpose and materials usage guidelines. Get a variety of glues and road test them. There are two-part epoxies, craft glues, slick-surface glues, fabric glues, cements, cyanocrylates. ... It's a never-ending story! You'll probably find that you gravitate toward a few workhorse glues, but don't let that stop you from experimenting.

### Laminates

I'd love to work with two-part resin and other heavy-duty laminates, but I have asthma and am unable to use things with intense odors. If you do use resin, you may find it's your best bet for sealing jewelry items. Other options work as well, including Diamond Glaze and Liquid Laminate.

### Découpage Medium

I'm a Mod Podge gal from way back. I love this stuff. It comes in different finishes and it really works. For moisture resistance and to prevent stickiness, you may want to give it a final coat with an acrylic sealant.

**④ Bits and Baubles**

Wander down the scrapbook aisles to find a huge array of fabulous paper you can use to make beads and pendants. Or you can use some of the wonderful papers for backgrounds in your collages. Chipboard, a heavy-duty, cardboard-like material, is a personal favorite, though it's important to seal it with a laminate to protect it. Another similar material is Grungeboard—I highly recommend it. Also in the scrapbooking aisle you'll find a wide selection of acrylic tiles and metal frames for collages.

**⑤ Ephemerally Yours**

Oh, how I love old paper. Ephemera refers to vintage paper objects, things that are ephemeral and fleeting but have somehow managed to survive the passage of time. Each piece of paper tells a small story, and when you use these bits of history in your work either by copying them or by using the actual items, your work takes on a new dimension. Ephemera can be found online, but I love treasure troving in antique malls, flea markets and thrift stores. I've been collecting bits of paper for more than twenty years now, and it never ceases to fascinate me.

**⑥ Newswire**

There are several kinds of wire used in jewelry making. Cabled steel wire is used primarily in bead stringing. It consists of multiple strands of stainless steel cabled together and coated in nylon. The higher the strand count, the more supple and strong the wire will be. Wire comes in a wide range of diameters—choose the right wire by making sure the wire fills the bead's hole.

Another type of wire commonly used for jewelry making is hard wire. It comes in base or precious metals. You can use it to make your own jump rings, clasps and jewelry components and to wrap around other items to secure them. The larger the gauge, the thinner the wire. Memory wire is tempered steel forged into a permanent shape. Use only memory wire shears to cut this wire. Cutting it with regular pliers will leave the wire razor-sharp, and it will dull your cutting tools.

# Tool Chest

A gal needs a few tools in her arsenal if she wants to get her craft on. This is a rundown of the tools I've featured in this book. Of course, this is just a smattering of the selections you'll find if you start to look—but you have to start somewhere, and this is where I recommend you start.

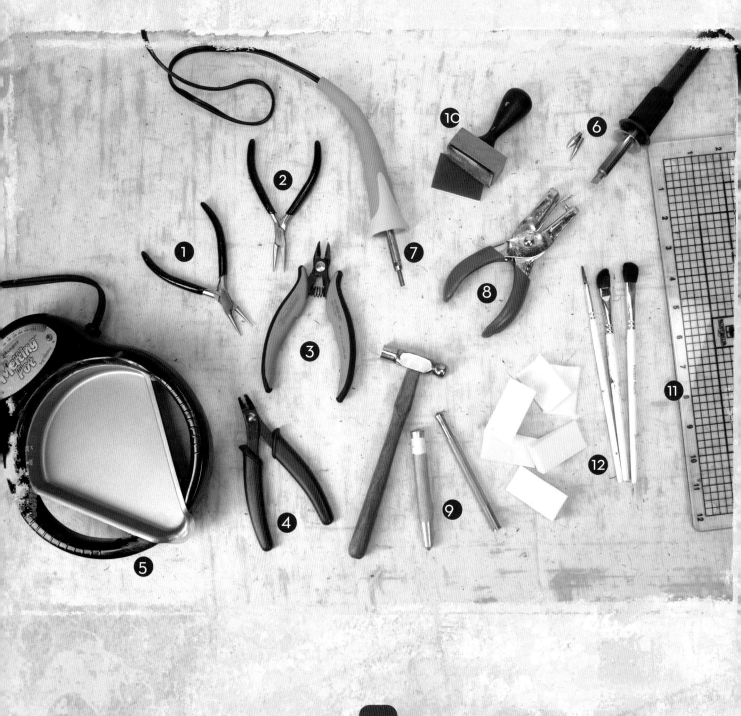

**① Round-Nose Pliers**

These pliers have round barrels and are used for creating loops and rounding hard wire.

**② Chain-Nose Pliers**

These pliers have flattened barrels and are used for grasping and forming hard wire.

**③ Wire Cutters**

There are a variety of wire cutters, and they each have different applications. Read the packaging to find out what wires and materials work best with each tool so you don't wreck the blades on your cutters. There is no real one-size-fits-all cutter tool.

**④ Crimp Tool**

Crimp tools have two chambers used to secure wire inside crimp beads and tubes. They come in three different sizes. Use the right size for your crimp beads and tubes.

**⑤ Melt Art Pot**

This electric-powered hot pot has heat settings for melting a variety of materials, including UTEE and wax. Clean the pot with a paper towel while it's still warm. Take care when using and cleaning this pot because it can get extremely hot. Use the handles on the sides when pouring.

**⑥ Soldering and Wood-Burning Tool**

If you want to do simple soldering, you'll need a soldering tool with a heated tip. Use a soldering tool in conjunction with solder (a filler metal) and flux (a lubricating medium that prevents oxidation) to join metal pieces. The tip of a soldering tool gets extraordinarily hot, so be careful. You may also purchase a multipurpose tool with a variety of interchangeable tips for soldering and wood burning. I bought mine from Walnut Hollow. You can use the wood-burning tip in several ways. Use the pointed tip to burn lines and patterns in wood. I used it to burn the edges of paper-covered wooden stars (see page 81).

**⑦ Hot-Fix Crystal Applicator**

The hot-fix crystal applicator is used to adhere flat-backed crystals to porous surfaces. It comes with different-sized tips to accommodate different sizes of crystals. This tool gets very hot, so use it with caution.

**⑧ Hole Punch**

A hole punch can be used to punch holes in chipboard, thin wood and metal. Punches come in a variety of shapes, sizes and strengths. They are also available in fancy shapes perfect for using with shrink plastic.

**⑨ Grommet Setter**

This tool is used with a small hammer to set metal grommets in leather, fabric and other surfaces. The metal cylinders come in a variety of sizes with different shaped tips.

**⑩ Ink Applicator Tool**

This tool makes it easy to apply inks to various surfaces. Both foam and felt applicators are available. Foam works well with dye-based inks, and felt is great for alcohol inks.

**⑪ Glass Cutting Board**

A glass cutting board makes a great surface to use when working with hot tools that might burn a desk or jeweler's bench. It's also a great base for cutting out materials with craft knives.

**⑫ Paintbrushes and Sponges**

These are other crafty staples, and I recommend you have a huge array of brushes in your coffers. I love sea sponges for applying inks and paints. Makeup sponges work well, too.

# Basic Techniques

Here's the 411 on the basic techniques you'll need to know to turn your new creations into finished jewelry. Good technique is crucial if you want to make jewelry that lasts. There is a lot of questionable information out there, but I'm determined to help people learn the right way to do things. So yes, I'm a bit of a stickler. Practice until you've mastered the basics—you'll be glad you did. I pinky-swear promise.

## Crimping Wire

The most common method for attaching wire to a clasp is "crimping." Using a small metal bead or tube and a crimp tool, you can make quick work of this task.

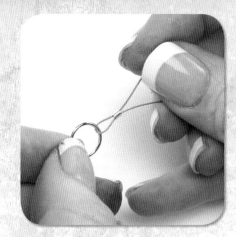

**1. Thread wire through crimp tube and clasp**

Thread the wire into the crimp tube, through the clasp and back through the crimp tube.

**2. Round crimp tube**

Place the tube inside the large hole at the front end of the tool and compress it into an oval shape. The oval shape helps keep the wires separated before the final crimping step.

**3. Flatten crimp tube**

Although the wires will want to cross, use your thumb to keep them uncrossed so you don't compromise the strength of the crimp-to-clasp connection. Place the oval tube into the indented hole at the back end of the tool and compress the tube, creating a separate chamber for each wire.

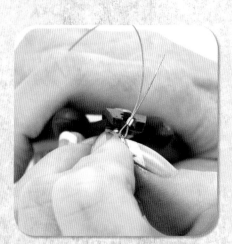

**4. Fold flattened tube in half**

Place the flattened crimp tube back into the large hole at the front end of the tool with the smooth side facing the inside jaws of the pliers. Compress the ends together, folding the tube in half.

**5. Trim excess wire**

Use wire cutters to cut the excess wire tail flush to the bottom of the crimped tube.

## Crimping wire with an EZ-Crimp end

Beadalon has created a new way of crimping that creates a seamless and clean finish for your designs. The EZ-Crimp end is a metal wire end that you attach to your wire using a special pair of pliers.

### 1. Thread wire into EZ-Crimp

Thread the end of the wire into the EZ-Crimp end. Place the EZ-Crimp end into the large hole at the front end of a Mighty Crimp tool. Align the shiny sides of the tube with the jaws of the pliers.

### 2. Squeeze EZ-Crimp

Compress the tube around the wire, working up and down the tube and pressing hard. Test the wire to be sure it is secure. Continue to squeeze until the wire is secure.

## Opening and Closing a Jump Ring

Opening and closing a jump ring properly is important if you want to keep your jewelry from falling apart easily. Use good-quality jump rings and follow these simple steps.

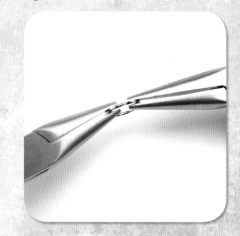

### 1. Grasp ring on either side of break

Grasp the jump ring on either side of the break in the tips of the jaws of 2 pairs of chain-nose pliers. (Or use a pair of bent-nose pliers.)

### 2. Open ring laterally

The key to opening a jump ring is to open the jaws in opposition to each other instead of outward from the center. If you open a jump ring by pulling the ends apart, the metal becomes stressed, and the circle loses its shape. Open the ring laterally so that 1 end is moving toward you and 1 end is moving away from you.

### 3. Close ring laterally

When you are ready to close the jump ring, grasp the ends in your pliers and move them past each other as you did before, gently compressing them together as you move them. Move the ends past each other again, but this time you should feel them click into place. This means you've created tension, and the jump ring should remain closed. If they don't click, keep passing them while gently compressing them together until they are secure.

## Turning a Loop

When creating dangles or beaded chains, you'll need to create wire loops.
Here's how to execute this simple maneuver.

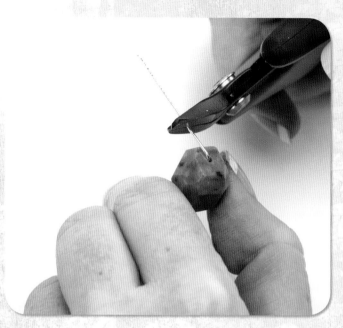

**1. Bend wire above bead**
After threading a bead onto a head pin, bend the wire at a
90° angle flush to the top of the bead.

**2. Trim wire**
Cut off the excess wire, leaving a ⅛" (3mm) tail.

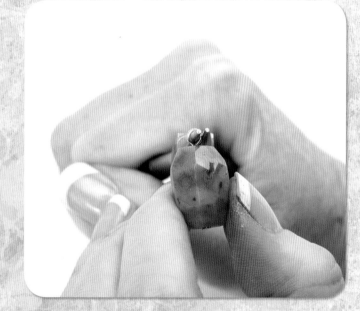

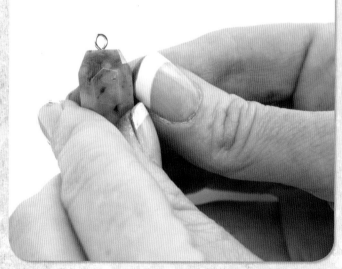

**3. Create loop**
Grasp the tail in the very front end of your round-nose pliers
and bend it over itself into a loop.

**Finished loop**
Your bead should have a round loop at the top when you
are finished. At first your loops may look more like p's than
o's, but with practice they will improve.

16

# Making a Wrapped Loop

For a more secure finish, create a coiled wire loop.
This takes practice, but it's well worth the effort.

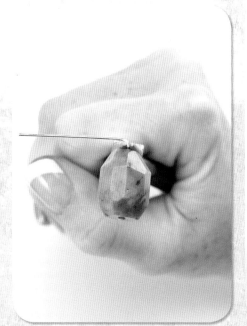

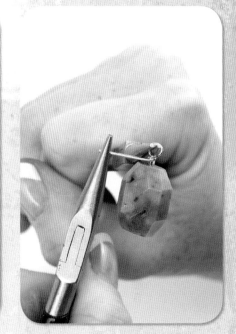

**1. Bend wire above bead**
Thread a bead onto a head pin, and grasp the wire at the top of the bead with round-nose pliers.

**2. Loop wire around pincer**
Use your fingers or a pair of chain-nose pliers to bend the wire around 1 of the pincers to form a loop.

**3. Twist wire around base of loop**
Use chain-nose pliers or your fingers to firmly coil the wire around the base of the loop until the coiled wire reaches the top of the bead.

**4. Trim away wire tail**
Cut off the excess wire with wire cutters.

**5. Tuck in wire end**
Use chain-nose pliers to tuck the remaining wire into the bottom of the coil.

# Making a Wire Hook

If you're in a pinch for a clasp, you can always make your own. This simple wire hook can double as an ear wire if you sand the exposed wire end. Make sure your wire gauge is thick enough for the hook to maintain its shape during regular use.

**1. Cut wire piece**
Cut a 4" (10cm) piece of 18-gauge (or higher) wire.

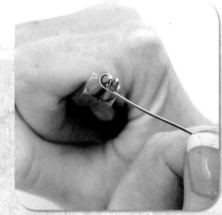

**2. Loop end of wire**
Grasp an end of the wire with round-nose pliers and turn a small loop.

**3. Create U shape**
Bend the wire over your pointer finger to create a 'u' shape.

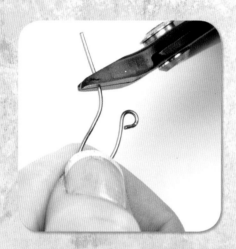

**4. Trim off end of wire**
Cut off the excess wire, leaving a ⅛" (3mm) tail.

**5. Bend wire tail**
Bend the wire tail slightly with your fingers or round-nose pliers.

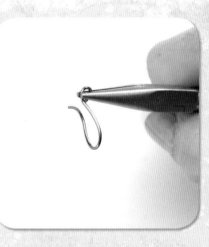

**6. Turn looped end perpendicular**
Use chain-nose pliers to bend the loop upward at a 90° angle from the front of the hook. Sand the wire end for comfort, if desired.

## Conditioning Polymer Clay

Polymer clay must be conditioned before use. Here's a method that helps make the process move a little faster. If you use a pasta machine to condition your clay, make sure to dedicate it exclusively to crafting. Once it has been used with clay, it shouldn't be used to make pasta.

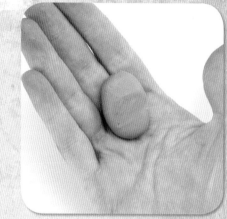

**1. Slice thin pieces of clay**
Cut off a small hunk of clay with a slicer tool.

**2. Run clay through pasta machine**
Place the clay into a pasta machine on 1 of the thickest settings and run it through. Continue to run the clay through the pasta machine, lowering the setting after each pass until the clay is suitably thin. If you will be cutting the clay into shapes, you may stop here.

**3. Knead clay with hands**
If you'll be forming the clay into dimensional shapes, knead it in your hands until it is soft and pliable.

## Drilling

A girl with a power tool need not rely on anyone else to turn just about anything into a cool piece of jewelry. You can do it; it's easy! Here's a quick look at the basics of drilling for the power-tool challenged.

Always use a block of wood as a base for the item you are going to drill. Mark your item before drilling to ensure proper placement of the hole. Hold the item down and drill your hole. Once you start drilling, you may find yourself looking for things to drill. It's easy and fun! Just make sure your drilled hole is large enough to accommodate a jump ring or wire.

# The Looking Glass

## Techniques for Working with Glass

When Alice went through the looking glass, she had some pretty interesting adventures. What might you discover if you went into the looking glass yourself? Glass can be a protective cover or a window, it can be filled or emptied, it can be tinted or decorated. It can provide a lovely frame within which your creative ideas might flourish. Here are some basic techniques to spark your creative fire.

In this chapter, I've used microscope-slide-style glass pieces to show you the techniques. You can take these same ideas and use them with recycled glass, beach glass, old cut-up bottles, glass-paneled reliquaries, flat-back glass stones...you see where I'm going with this? Check out the embossing technique in *Stained* (see page 26) to learn how to create the look of stained glass with a stamp and some embossing powder. Use etching cream, foil tape, solder and transparencies to make a layered frame you can solder and ink to look like a vintage treasure in *Come Up and See My Etchings* (see page 30). Try these same techniques with acrylic and see how the look of the finished piece changes.

# Vogue Slide

*If you've been wanting to try working with microscope-style glass slides, but the idea of soldering is intimidating, this technique is an easy way to get the same effect. Vintage Vogue pattern catalog images are wonderful for a variety of paper crafts. Remember that each pendant will be unique, unless you opt to scan and copy. I like using the original—it's like capturing history. Choose beads to match the ink colors you use to fill in the image. I fell in love with these frosted black stone tubes from GreatCraftWorks, and to break them up I used cloisonné beads and Swarovski crystals. Experiment with sliding all kinds of artwork into these miniature wearable frames.*

## Materials

vintage Vogue pattern image

memory glass slide and memory glass frame (Ranger)

ink pens in Rust and Pesto (Adirondack by Ranger)

Swarovski crystals in coordinating colors:

    3 5mm olivine rounds

    3 6mm copper crystal rondelles

    2 4mm jet AB rounds

10mm silver-plated oval jump ring (Beadalon)

6mm silver-plated jump ring (Beadalon)

**Tools:** scissors, round-nose pliers, 2 pairs chain-nose pliers

## Creating a Microscope Slide Pendant

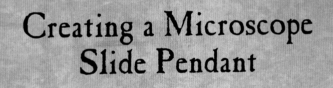

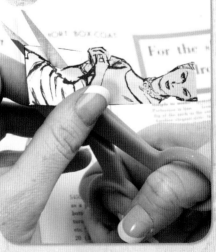

### 1. Select image

Select an image of your choice. You may either use an original image or scan the image and print a copy. Place a glass slide on top of the image and position the image under the glass. Trace around the slide.

### 2. Cut out silhouette

Carefully cut around the image, retaining as much detail as possible and keeping straight edges on the top, bottom and 1 side of the paper.

### 3. Color image

Color in the image with ink pens.

### 4. Slide glass and image into frame

Sandwich the image between 2 glass slides and insert it into the frame. Close the frame.

### 5. Link jump ring to slide

Link an oval jump ring to the top of the slide. (See Techniques, page 15, for instructions on opening and closing a jump ring.)

### 6. Add beaded dangles

Create dangles with beads and attach them to a smaller jump ring with pliers. (See Techniques, page 16, for instructions on making dangles.) Link the jump ring with the dangles to the oval jump ring.

*The important thing with these tiny cutout images is that they fill the frame and still allow for some empty spaces. It's also important that you do a good job cutting them out. You may have to scan and shrink the image you want to use so it will fit. Once you've created your pendant, choose interesting beads in coordinating colors to complement it.*

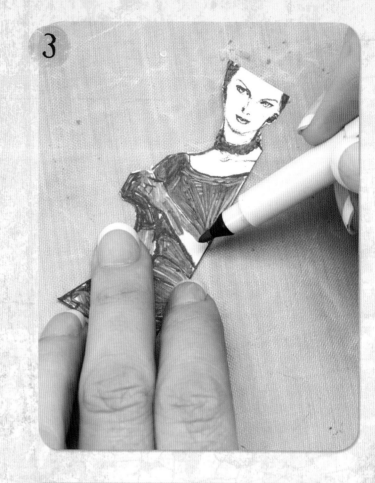

# *Gallery*

### Vogue Earrings

These simple earrings are the perfect complement to the *Vogue Slide* necklace. Just pick a few of the same beads used in your necklace and whip up some matching earrings.

### Vogue Again

Since I used the original image from the pattern book in my pendant, I had to use a different one to recreate it in the step-by-step photos. As you can see, the slight variation gives the finished design a slightly different appeal. If you want to scan your images to make more than one of the same pendant, you can opt to do so.

### More Vogue

This technique is incredibly versatile. Change the look and scale of your piece by choosing a square slide instead of a rectangular one.

You may also play around with the beads you use to complement your framed art. The combination of strong black, soft purple and neutral green makes this necklace feel so retro. It took awhile to get the scale right, but I really, really like it now. This glass frame is from HHH Enterprises and has a slide clasp mechanism to make it easy to change things out. I chose to make it a permanent fixture by using UHU clear glue to secure the image. You can opt to copy, size and print out your image and then color it in, but first test your inks out on the paper you choose to see how they react.

# Stained

Embossing powder works on many surfaces, including glass. It comes in many different colors, so there is no end to the looks you can create with this surprisingly simple technique. Here I colored a stamped and embossed image with inks to create the look of stained glass. Gather up a pile of patterned stamps, embossing powders and alcohol inks and have a blast! To create a necklace with my pendant, I added vintage Lucite beads, Swarovski crystals and channel chain in colors that coordinated with the vivid yellow, red and black of the stained design.

## Materials

*memory glass square slides and memory glass frames (Ranger)*

*patterned background rubber stamps*

*black embossing powder (Ranger)*

*alcohol inks in Red Pepper and Butterscotch (Ranger)*

*embossing pad (Big and Bossy)*

*1 12mm acid green Lucite bead (The Beadin' Path)*

*3 3mm jet Swarovski rounds*

*3 20-gauge sterling head pins (Beadalon)*

*1 20-gauge sterling ball-tipped head pin (Beadalon)*

*5mm sterling jump ring (Beadalon)*

*4mm sterling jump ring (Beadalon)*

*dryer sheet*

**Tools:** *small paintbrush, heat-setting tool, round-nose pliers, 2 pairs chain-nose pliers*

## Embossing Glass

### 1. Stamp slide
Clean the glass slide with a dryer sheet to prevent static electricity. Select the section of the stamp you wish to highlight by holding the glass against the stamp. Ink the stamp with embossing medium. Stamp the design by placing the glass flat on the stamp and pressing down.

### 2. Pour on powder
Pour embossing powder onto the wet medium. Tap the excess powder into the jar.

### 3. Melt powder with heat tool

Use a heat tool to melt the powder until the powder becomes glossy and wet looking. Work from the top to the bottom of the slide, keeping the heat tool moving as you work. Allow the glass to cool.

### 4. Color in details

Use a fine paintbrush and alcohol inks to color in the details of the stamp. Allow the ink to dry.

### 5. Secure glass inside frame

To create a pendant, place the stamped glass against a second glass piece with the embossed side of the glass facing the second piece of glass. Slide the 2 glass pieces into the frame and close it.

### 6. Add dangles

Create 3 coiled dangles with jet beads and regular head pins and 1 coiled dangle with a Lucite bead and a ball-tipped head pin. Attach all of the dangles to a small jump ring. (See Techniques, page 17, for instructions on making coiled dangles.) Attach the small jump ring and the pendant to a larger jump ring with chain-nose pliers.

*tip*

*Getting this to work just right is a little tricky. You may need to practice, and you'll definitely need to use a bold stamp with simple lines and empty spaces you can fill in with ink. I recommend dusting the embossing powder residue off the glass with a very small paintbrush before setting the design with the heat tool. No matter what, there will be a little bit of fleck-ing. You can scrape some of that off with a razor blade and try to live with the rest!*

# Gallery

### Stained Chick

With the flourishes stamp, the embossing technique looks quite elegant, but you can also use it with a cuter image for a completely different effect.

### Optically Stained

This image stamped in all black comes from one of the Hero Arts Mixed Design clear stamps. It's embossed on the back of a vintage optical lens. Because this is a single pane of glass, I sealed it with some Diamond Glaze to prevent the embossed areas from chipping. The gunmetal chain is from Blue Moon Beads, and I've accented the pendant with freshwater pearls and a black diamond 8mm Swarovksi round. Try this embossing technique on all kinds of glass.

### Stained Earrings

You can use the same technique on acrylic to make these lovely and less fragile earrings!

# Come Up and See My Etchings

It may not seem like much of a pickup line now, but when a gentleman at the turn of the twentieth century invited a lady to "Come up and see his etchings," he was actually suggesting a romantic interlude, luring the woman in with promises of fine art. In this piece, vintage ladies float inside each glass charm. The soldered glass is etched with the application of a special cream over a stencil. The protected parts remain raised, and the exposed places respond to the cream to create an etched appearance. Ink is used along the frames to create the look of antique copper. Sheer magic! To create the finished necklace as shown, I linked the pendant to a length of copper chain with a filigreed butterfly component and created my own clasp from sixteen-gauge copper wire. I added some Swarovski crystal accents to complement the connected etched glass pieces.

## Materials

1" (3cm) memory glass square (Ranger)
foil tape
lead-free silver solder
flux
transparency sheets
Glass Etch cream
Glass Etch butterfly stencils
alcohol inks in Black and Rust (Ranger)
silver-plated jump rings
thin marker
felt
rubber gloves

**Tools:** *paintbrush, soldering tool, clamps to hold glass while soldering, ink applicator tool, scissors, bone folder*

## Etching Glass

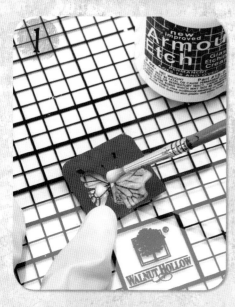

### 1. Apply Glass Etch
Peel the back off the stencil and adhere it to the glass. Wearing rubber gloves, use a paintbrush to apply Glass Etch to the glass, allowing it to set for 1 minute. (Wear gloves to prevent the cream from damaging your skin.)

### 2. Wash off Glass Etch
Wash off the Glass Etch and remove the stencil. Wash away any remaining cream. Let the glass dry.

### 3. Trace around image
Place the glass slide on top of a transparency sheet and trace around it with a thin marker.

### 4. Cut out image
Cut out the image, making sure it fits the glass square exactly.

### 5. Adhere foil tape to glass
Clean any fingerprints from the transparency sheet and the glass. Sandwich the image between 2 glass slides, keeping the etched side of the glass on top. Adhere foil tape around the edges of the sandwiched image.

### 6. Smooth out foil tape
Use a bone folder to smooth out the foil tape.

## *tip*

*You may use virtually any stencil you like for this technique. Try out this etching technique on any glass surface, including flat-back glass stones or even cut and tumbled recycled glass. I love the look of a transparency that is slightly hidden by the etching, but you can opt to keep the glass clear. See how things might change depending on the inks or frames you choose.*

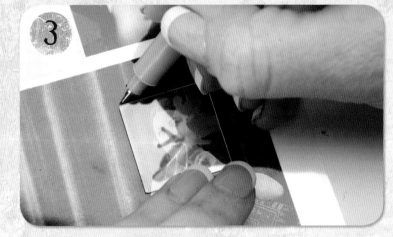

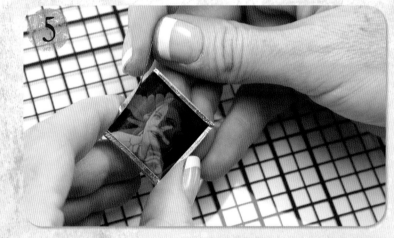

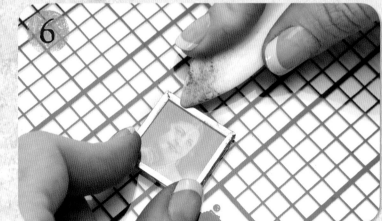

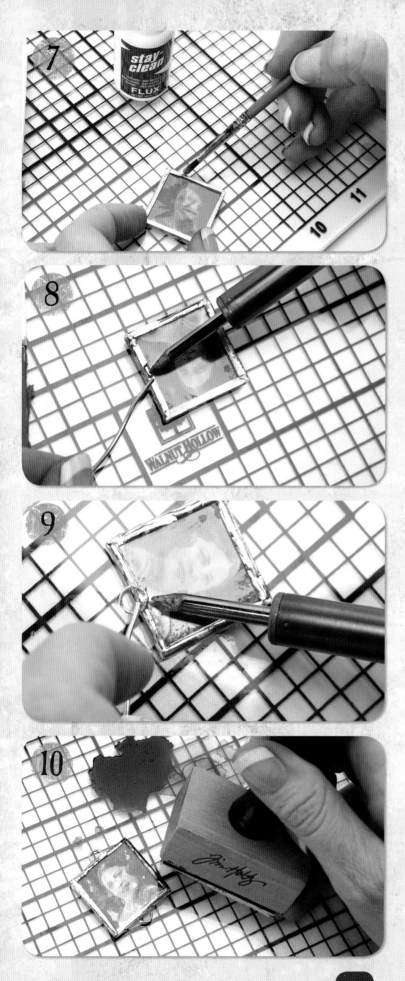

### 7. Apply flux

Use a paintbrush to apply flux to the foil tape.

### 8. Apply solder

Hold lead-free silver solder to the tip of the heated soldering tool directly above the foil tape. As the solder liquifies, it will adhere to the foil tape. Solder the front and back of all sides of the sandwiched glass squares.

### 9. Solder jump ring to pendant

Solder a jump ring to the top center of the pendant. If you'll be linking another etched pendant to this one, you may solder a jump ring to the bottom center of the pendant as well.

### 10. Apply ink to soldered edges

Use the ink applicator tool to dab black and rust ink onto the soldered edges to create an antiqued copper finish on the frame of the charm and the jump ring. Allow the ink to dry.

# Resist This

Alcohol inks can be used to color glass, and if you use this clever resist technique, you can have both inked places and negative space. I learned this technique from Tim Holtz at Ranger U, and I find it endlessly fun. You can give more dimension to the design by inking the paper behind it with matching or coordinating rubber stamps. Add some simple wire wrapping for dimension or leave it plain—it's totally up to you! To make a necklace with my resist pendant, I strung a length of memory wire with Czech volcano glass beads from York Novelty that were similar in variegation and coloration to the layered inks in the pendant. The pendant is linked to the beaded wire with a simple jump ring.

## Materials

1" × 3" (3cm × 8cm) memory glass slides and frames with black patina (Ranger)

alcohol inks in Pesto and Stonewashed (Ranger)

swirl stamp (Inkadinkado 96253-P)

Old French Writing stamp (Hero Arts H2365)

jet black archival ink

1 pewter hummingbird charm

Glossy Accents paper (Ranger)

20-gauge silver-plated ColourCraft wire (Beadalon)

2 5mm silver-plated jump rings (Beadalon)

**Tools:** ink-blending tool, alcohol ink applicator, blending felt, round-nose pliers, 2 pairs chain-nose pliers, nipper tool, heat tool, scissors, paper towels

## Creating a Resist with Alcohol Ink

### 1. Ink glass slides
Use the applicator tool to dab inks onto the glass slide. No 2 slides will be the same—just keep dabbing until you get something you like. The more you dab, the heavier the color. Twist and turn the applicator to vary the ink placement. Allow the ink to dry. Use a heat tool to speed up the drying process if you're impatient like me.

### 2. Stamp slide
Ink a bold, simple stamp with black archival ink and stamp the pre-inked glass.

## 3. Wipe away ink

Quickly wipe off the ink with a paper towel to create a resist of the stamped image. If you don't create a resist or you don't like how it turned out, redo it. I stamped the glass at the top and bottom from several angles.

## 4. Stamp paper

Stamp a piece of Glossy Accents paper to fit the frame. Stamp the top and bottom of the paper as you did with the glass to create a coordinating swirl. Place the glass into position and trace around it.

## 5. Stamp center of paper

Stamp the center of the paper with a script stamp or a different image. Remember that it's being filtered through inked glass so it needs to be bold. Cut the stamped paper using the lines you traced in step 4.

## 6. Ink frame

Ink the frame to coordinate with the glass using your blending tool. Allow the ink to dry. Sandwich the inked paper between the inked glass and a second blank piece of glass with the inked side of the glass face down. Insert the glass and paper into the frame and close it.

## 7. Wrap slide with wire

To create the pendant as shown, wrap wire around the slide and create tension by tucking the wire and bending it with round-nose pliers. Be careful not to wrap too tightly so the glass doesn't break.

## 8. Add charm

Attach a dangle to the wire if you like. (See Techniques, pages 16–17 for instructions on turning and wrapping loops to make dangles.) I used a small pewter hummingbird on a 5mm jump ring. Add a 5mm jump ring to the top of your pendant so you can attach it to a chain or to a beaded design.

*tip*

*Try using this technique with image stamps. I have a tiny coffee cup stamp that looks great in resist. Make sure you wipe the ink off quickly to get a good resist. If you let the ink sit for too long, it might not work as well.*

# *Gallery*

### Poppy Resist

In this version, an entirely different color palette creates design appeal. I love brown and blue together—it's always a winning combination. I inked with Mushroom, created the resist with an Inkadinkado harlequin stamp, and stamped the Gloss Paper on the inside with another Hero Arts Mixed Design clear stamp. The necklace is made of smoky quartz faceted coins, pacific opal and smoky quartz Swarovski crystals and one tiny freshwater pearl to pull the cream color out of the pendant and into the necklace. I added a bold circle chain for a second layer.

### Purple Resist

This piece is for those who are passionate about purple. To create this vibrant shade, I inked the stamped image with layers of Eggplant and Wild Plum alcohol inks. I created a resist by stamping the glass with a Hero Arts Mixed Design clear stamp in a dotted swirl design. I inked the inside with the same stamp and closed the frame. I felt the scale of the pendant called for a bold necklace, so I beaded a strand of violet AB 4mm Swarovski bicones and added a thin paper-clip-style silver chain from Bead Trust. The ends are finished with Beadalon EZ-Crimps. Then I secured it all together with Beadalon Colourcraft purple silver-plated wire. A tiny satin bow at the top pulls it all together perfectly.

# Plastic Fantastic

## Techniques for Working with Plastic

Plastic is highly underrated and underappreciated as far as jewelry-making materials go. As a designer, I'm open to any material that catches my eye, and I don't cotton much to materials snobbery. Plastic is an endlessly interesting medium—you might be surprised at just how much fun it is! I collect vintage plastic Lucite and Bakelite beads that I love to mix with fine materials in unexpected ways. Plastic is so lightweight you can get huge looks that aren't heavy to wear, and that's a mighty good thing if you ask me, since I like to wear gimungous jewelry and all. Even if you prefer your jewelry on a smaller scale, plastic is a wonderful chameleon-like material I highly suggest you explore.

Inked plastic can be sealed with a clear medium to allow the light to come through and the ink to stay on, but in *Breathe In, Breathe Out* (see page 42) a découpaged backdrop creates depth and dimension. Melted UTEE can be swirled in various colors or pigments and poured into molds to make charms and components. In *Buddhalicious* (see page 50), a carved gemstone bead is molded and turned into a Technicolor celebration. And check out the *Glitterati* project (see page 54) for an UTEE glitter tip. This chapter also explores the joys of shrink plastic and stamped, inked dominoes. Get your plastic on, baby!

# Nice and Naughty

## Materials

Naughty French Spot
Illustrations (Dover)

shrink plastic (Rough and
Ready by PolyShrink)

ink marker in Red Pepper
(Adirondack by Ranger)

fine-tipped permanent black marker
(Micron .005 by Kuretake)

4mm gunmetal jump rings
(Rings & Things)

silver-plating pen (Krylon)

**Tools:** hole punch, heat tool or
toaster oven, metal spatula,
2 pairs chain-nose pliers, scissors

*A*re you a wicked girl? Do you love to dance on the edge of decency? Do you rouge your knees and roll your
stockings down? Well, my little flapper girl, these nifty shrink art charms are certain to suit your style.
Vo dee oh doh! If vintage ladies aren't your thing, you can stamp or draw any image of your choice onto shrink plastic.
When choosing an image, anticipate the finished size—remember, shrink plastic shrinks by between 20 and 40 percent.
I used jump rings to link my shrink art charms to a length of gunmetal chain overflowing with Siam and jet Swarovksi
crystals to create an Art Deco appeal.

# Creating Dangles with Shrink Plastic

### 1. Trace images onto shrink plastic
Select several images from the Dover art book. Remember that the images will shrink significantly, so pick large, detailed images for best results. Trace the images onto the rough side of a sheet of shrink plastic using a fine-tipped permanent black marker.

### 2. Add red accents
Use a fine-tipped red ink marker to color some of the details of each image.

### 3. Cut out images
Use sharp scissors to cut around the images, making interesting shapes.

### 4. Make holes in each piece
Use a hole punch to make a hole at the top of each piece.

### 5. Shrink images
Use a heat tool to shrink each image, moving the heat tool constantly as the pieces shrink. If necessary, use a metal spatula to flatten each piece before it cools completely. Or shrink the images by placing them in a pre-heated toaster oven on top of a brown paper bag liner on an oven tray. Allow the pieces to cool.

### 6. Apply silver ink to the edges of each piece
Use a silver-plating pen to edge the images. Allow the pieces to dry. Link each charm to a length of chain with a jump ring. (See Techniques, page 15, for instructions on opening and closing a jump ring.)

## Gallery

### Sugar and Spice Earrings and Pendant

For these fun little pieces, I used images traced from a 1940s *Vogue* sewing magazine to trace the images and then filled them in with colored pencils. Attach the pendants to necklaces or zippers. I edged these with gold leafing pen and added coordinated Swarovski crystal accents on Beadalon star-tipped head pins. Remember to punch as many holes as you'll need for the finished piece before shrinking the plastic.

## tip

*Any clean, simple black-and-white inked illustrations will work here. The bigger the better so you can really get the detail in before it shrinks! It's important to use a very, very fine-tipped marker so you can get the lines clean, or the finished result could lack definition. You can add more or less color depending on your mood.*

# Breathe In, Breathe Out

*I*n the stress of our day-to-day lives, it's easy to forget to breathe. This chunky yet lightweight pendant gently reminds us: Breathe in. Breathe out. Wash, rinse, repeat. Plastic is so clear and lightweight, you can create many different effects by applying inks in varied colors to all kinds of plastic pieces. I created a striking necklace to showcase this chunky pendant by making it the focal point of a rosary-style chain of linked funky acrylic beads.

## Materials

large faceted clear acrylic star

sticky note printed with "Breathe in, Breathe out" (Stik-Withit brand) or computer-generated printed version

pack of pink patterned tissue paper with heart-print psychedelic paper (Décopatch)

alcohol inks in Rust and Terra Cotta (Ranger)

glossy découpage medium (Mod Podge by Plaid)

**Tools:** *scissors, alcohol ink applicator tool, felt*

## Inking Dimensional Plastic

1

Things I need to do today:
1. Breathe in.
2. Breathe out.

### 1. Cut out phrase
Cut out the words you'd like to use on your star with small, sharp scissors. You may cut the words directly from a sticky note or a printed page or type up the phrase of your choice on the computer and print it out.

## 2. Adhere phrase to back of star

Adhere the cutout words to the back of the star using découpage medium. Allow it to dry.

## 3. Apply alcohol ink

Use the Ranger alcohol ink applicator tool and felt to pounce ink onto the back of the star. Be sparing with the ink—a little goes a long way!

## 4. Adhere tissue paper to star back

Paint the back of the star with découpage medium and place the star on top of a piece of tissue paper, placing the heart almost in the center of the back of the star.

## 5. Tear paper away from edges

While the paper is still wet, gently rip around the edges of the star to fray the paper. Don't allow the paper edges to overlap the edge of the star. Allow the découpage medium to dry.

## 6. Seal paper

Paint a thin layer of découpage medium over the tissue paper. Use your fingers to smooth the paper down flush to the points of the star. Allow the medium to dry.

*tip*

*Acrylic makes a great surface for alcohol inks, but if you don't seal the ink, it may not stay where you put it. You can opt to use a clear sealer (non-alcohol-based), or you can découpage the ink to protect it.*

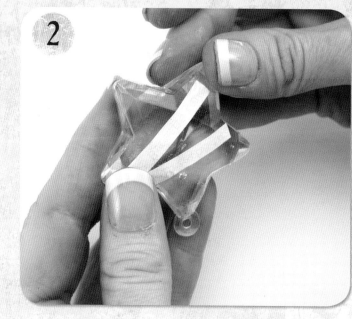

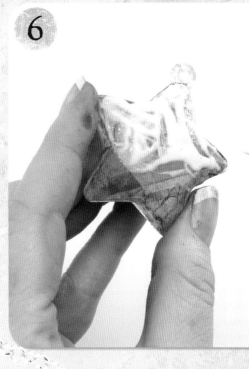

# *Gallery*

## Framed

This acrylic and metal lantern frame came from ARTchix Studio. I inked the panels with layers of Adirondack alcohol inks in Mushroom, Bottle and silver mixative. After adding the silver, I dripped on a tiny bit of Mushroom ink and dabbed it off with a foam wedge. I used torn pages from a vintage French dictionary and accented the top of the lantern with miniature watch parts. You can add more charms to this simple copper bracelet as you learn new techniques, but I rather like its stark simplicity.

## Pour Vous

Ink on plastic, oh what fun! In this version, I inked a simple white paper backdrop and added a printed French phrase. I'm digging the vibrant alcohol inks I used here: stream, Oregano and Red Pepper. I sealed the design with découpage medium and edged it with metallic pen for a more finished look. It's all hanging from the new Beadalon Quick Links components. *Tres chic, n'est pas?*

# Make a Wish

A richly detailed stamp, a drilled plastic domino and two green-hued inks and glazes come together to create a rich and sumptuous focal element that makes a great necklace pendant. Once you get started, you won't be able to stop. Plastic dominoes are great mini canvases for your artwork. Whatever medium you choose, be sure to seal your work with a thick coat of glaze. Get thee to the domino store and quick! I hung this pendant on a strand of olive Swarovski crystals that perfectly matches the shade of the ink used on the domino. A small marcasite-encrusted bead set off by AB crystal rounds adds a bit of asymmetry and whimsy.

## Materials

standard plastic off-white domino

tin can mail stamp (Inkadinkado)

jet black archival ink (Ranger)

alcohol inks in Gold, Butterscotch and Terra Cotta (Ranger)

Glossy Accents (Ranger)

18k silver-plating pen (Krylon)

**Tools:** electric drill with ¹⁄₁₆" (2mm) bit, alcohol ink applicator tool, heat tool

## Creating a Collage on a Domino

### 1. Apply ink to domino
Apply ink to both ends of the ink applicator tool (leave the center or the applicator clean of ink).

### 2. Blend inks
Use the non-inked center of the tool to blend the ink blots into a more subtle variegation of color.

### 3. Stamp image onto domino

Select an image to stamp onto the domino. Use an applicator tool to dab inks onto the stamp, layering the colors until you achieve the desired effect. Press the stamp firmly onto the inked domino, placing the image as desired.

### 4. Set ink with heat tool

Use a heat tool to dry and set the ink.

### 5. Edge domino with silver

Once the ink has dried, edge the domino with the silver-plating pen. If desired, you may also color the back of the domino with a silver pen.

### 6. Create silver frame

Hold the silver pen at an angle and create a thin silver frame around the edges of the domino.

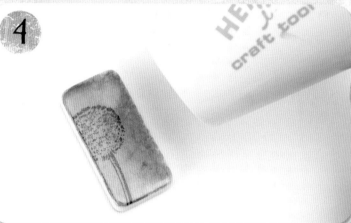

### 7. Apply protective coating

Carefully apply Glossy Accents over the front of the image, avoiding the pen edge. Allow the pendant to dry completely overnight.

### 8. Drill hole in pendant

If you'd like to make the domino into a pendant, use a pen to mark the placement of the hole at the top of the pendant. Drill through the marked spot using an electric drill.

**7**

**8**

## Gallery

### Who Me?

This fabulous flapper stamp from Dana Kovaks for Hampton Art Stamps has a bit of a Gustav Klimt influence. Since flappers and Klimt paintings are two of my favorite things, this stamp is about as perfect as can be. I used caramel-colored inks to create the background, which gives the design a more brooding look. The asymmetrical necklace includes dyed jade, Peruvian opal, faceted smoky quartz coins and large carnelian nuggets.

# Buddhalicious

*I*f these candy-colored Buddhas weren't made of UTEE, why they'd be good enough to eat! Yummy! Mix the mini Buddhas with chains and Swarovski crystals, and you've got a really fabulous and fun conversation starter. UTEE is a type of melt-and-pour plastic compound that comes in a rainbow of colors. It's super easy to use, and the design possibilities are truly endless. Almost anything becomes a mold—use your imagination. The rainbow shades of these UTEE Buddhas look great hanging in color spectrum order from this heavy gunmetal chain. I added crystal dangles in coordinating colors to tie the whole design together.

## Materials

UTEE Britz in Pink, Orange, Blue, Green, White (Ranger)

UTEE in Clear (Ranger)

Perfect Pearls Pigment embossing powder in pastel shades (Ranger)

Mold n' Pour (Ranger)

bead to mold (I used a Buddha bead)

20-gauge silver-plated Colourcraft wire (Beadalon)

**Tools:** melting pot, round-nose pliers, chain-nose pliers, flush cutters, silicon spatula, nonstick craft sheet, paper towels

## Making Molded Beads with Ultra-Thick Embossing Enamel

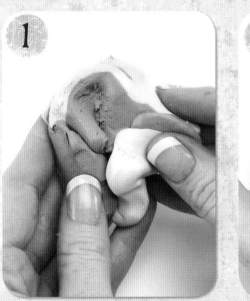

### 1. Begin mixing Mold n' Pour components
Mix equal amounts of the 2 Mold n' Pour components in your hands.

### 2. Finish mixing Mold n' Pour components
Continue mixing the 2 components together until the colors are completely blended.

### 3. Make mold

Press the bead into the mold material with enough pressure that the entire impression is embedded in the mold material. However, be careful not to press so hard that the bead breaks through the bottom of the mold material. Use your fingers to form the sides of the mold around the top of the bead. Allow the mold to harden for up to 1 minute. When your fingernails no longer leave an indention in the mold, it is ready to use.

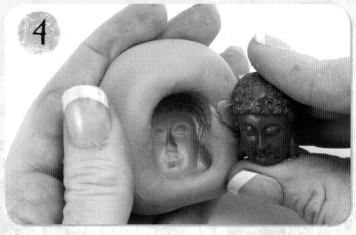

### 4. Remove bead from mold

Once the mold has set, remove the bead. You should see a clear impression of the object you used to make the mold.

### 5. Melt and mix UTEE mixture

Heat the melting pot to the temperature indicated on the package of UTEE. Pour 1 color of UTEE and clear UTEE in a 1/3 to 2/3 ratio into the melting pot. Add a sprinkle of embossing powder to the pot in a coordinating color. Allow the UTEE to melt, stirring it gently with a silicon spatula. Don't stir too much, or bubbles will form.

### 6. Form wire bail

While the UTEE is melting, cut a 2" (5cm) piece of wire. Bend an end of the wire into a short zigzag. Bend the wire at a 90° angle to form a bail for the pendant.

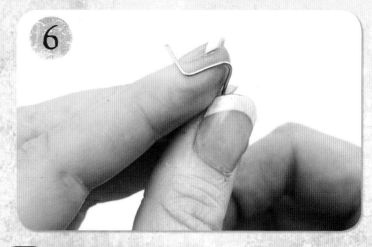

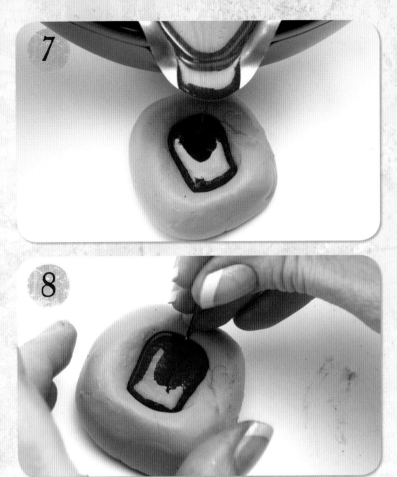

**7**

### 7. Pour UTEE into mold
When the UTEE is completely melted, pour it into your mold, filling it all the way to the top.

### 8. Insert wire bail into UTEE
Slip the wire bail into the UTEE, centering it at the top of the bead and pushing it into the center of the bead so it doesn't poke through the front or the back of the bead. Hold the bail in place until it stays by itself. Allow the UTEE to harden completely (approximately 5 minutes).

### 9. Remove bead from mold
Remove the UTEE bead from the mold.

### 10. Cut away any imperfections
Use flush cutters to trim away any imperfections around the edges of the bead.

### 11. Create bail at top of bead
Make a wrapped loop above the bead. (See Techniques, page 17, for instructions on making a wrapped loop.)

**8**

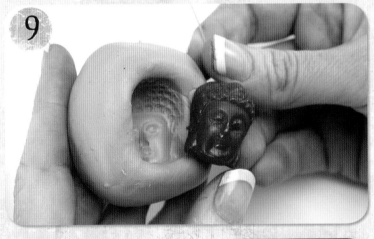

**9**

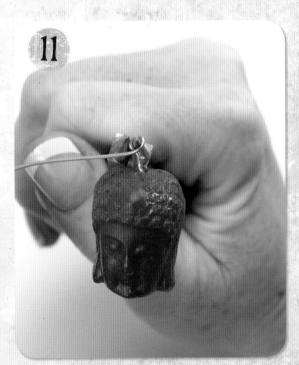

**11**

**10**

# Glitterati

*I* discovered something interesting while I was experimenting with UTEE. I had been trying to add glitter into the UTEE with no success—it just melted. But when I dusted the mold with fine glitter (I used Art Institute Glitter) before I poured in the UTEE, I ended up with a gorgeous shimmery, sparkly effect! Just brush any loose glitter away once you've popped the bead from the mold. Enjoy this new UTEE technique and add glitter to all your molded UTEE beads. Viva la sparkle! Chrysolite Swarovski crystal accents bring these earrings to life. I connected the beads to the ear wires with a double-looped 6mm peridot bicone.

## Materials

*UTEE Britz in green (Ranger)*

*Perfect Pearls Pigment embossing powder in Gold (Ranger)*

*green glitter (Art Institute Caribbean Collection)*

*Mold n' Pour (Ranger)*

*bead to mold*

*head pin*

*20-gauge silver-plated ColourCraft wire (Beadalon)*

**Tools:** *melting pot, round-nose pliers, chain-nose pliers, flush cutters, silicon spatula, nonstick craft sheet, paper towels*

## Making Molded Glitter Beads with Ultra-Thick Embossing Enamel

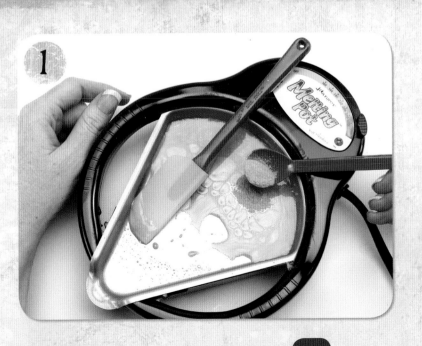

### 1. Mix striated UTEE

Follow steps 1 through 5 in the *Buddhalicious* project (see pages 51–52) for instructions on making a mold and mixing/melting UTEE. I used a locust bead to make my mold. When the UTEE is fully melted and mixed, add a generous scoop of Perfect Pearls gold embossing powder.

## 2. Fold in gold powder

Use a spatula to gently fold the gold powder into the melted UTEE. Don't overmix—you want to create a striated effect.

## 3. Dust mold with glitter

Pour glitter into your mold.

## 4. Tap out excess glitter

Gently tap the mold against your work surface to remove excess glitter, leaving a thin, even layer of glitter along the surface of the mold.

## 5. Pour UTEE into mold

Pour the UTEE into the mold, filling it to the top. Insert a head pin into the wet UTEE and hold it in place until the UTEE sets. Allow the UTEE to harden completely (approximately 5 minutes).

## 6. Make bead

Remove the UTEE bead from the mold.

## 7. Remove bead from mold

Wipe away any excess glitter. Make the bead into a dangle.

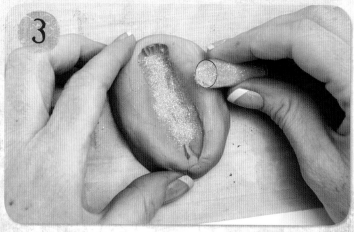

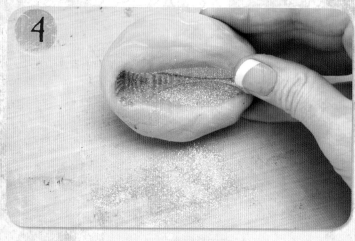

## Gallery

### Glitter Bones

This glittered skull was made using the same glittered UTEE technique as for the *Glitterati* earrings. The base is pearl UTEE with a dash of Perfect Pearls in Pearl. The mold was made from a ceramic Peruvian skull bead. The ceramic bone beads are also from Peru, and I've glittered them with a touch of Stardust Stickles.

# Cyber Crafty

## Techniques for Incorporating Digital Images

Five years ago I got my first computer, and it became my trusty companion and helpmate as I built my career. It was a long and winding road, and I'm still learning every day. Now I know my way around a scanner, photo-editing software and a publishing program. My love of ephemera has led me to learn these things so I can use the same fabulous image again and again and not lose it in one design. This is a chapter for those of you who are, like me, still learning the nuances of basic computer crafting. I think it's the wave of the future, and I've always been one for getting my surfboard ready at the first sign of big waves. Think of all of the cool things you can make if you can enlarge and shrink images or change them to different colors with just the click of a mouse.

In *Sew Buttons* (see page 60), an oversized metal bottle cap provides the frame for a miniature collage featuring a vintage *Vogue* sewing catalog image. I cut out, scanned, sized, printed and collaged this image as quick as you can say "Jack Sprat." Okay, maybe not quite that quickly, but you get the idea. There's nothing quite as ironic as using modern technology to make something that looks vintage. In *Lettres D'Amour* (see page 64) you'll use scanned vintage Victorian papers to make a miniature book/pendant. Ready, set, click!

# Sew Buttons

## Materials

*faux bottle cap (Maya Road)*

*vintage image*

*antique button*

*Stickles in Turquoise and Stardust (Ranger)*

*Liquid Laminate (Beacon)*

*2 9mm × 6mm blue topaz CRYSTALLIZED – Swarovski Elements teardrops*

*1 6mm pacific opal CRYSTALLIZED – Swarovski Elements rondelle*

*2 12mm silver-plated jump rings (Rings & Things)*

*1 4mm silver-plated jump ring (Rings & Things)*

*4 silver-plated head pins (Rings & Things)*

*1 silver-plated pin back (Rings & Things)*

*Amazing Goop*

*craft glue*

**Tools:** *computer with photo-editing software, scanner, printer, handheld electric drill with ⅛" (3mm) bit, 2 pairs chain-nose pliers, round-nose pliers, flush cutters, magic marker to mark hole placement, scissors*

To make this brooch, I've scanned and sized a vintage image from a *Vogue* sewing book and then adhered it inside a large faux bottle cap. Sparkles, ink and a vintage button create a charming mini collage. Add a pin back, some jump rings and crystals for a flirty little pin/pendant that's sure to please. Manipulating digital images is really so simple—you can use this technique to make any image you like just the right size and shape.

# Creating a Mini Collage with a Digitally Altered Image

## 1. Drill holes in bottle cap

Mark and drill holes in the top and bottom inside edge of the bottle cap.

## 2. Adhere image and button

Scan, size and print an image. I've used an image from a vintage *Vogue* sewing catalog, but you can choose any image you wish. Cut the image into a circle that fits into the bottle cap. Adhere the image to the inside of the bottle cap using craft glue. Allow it to dry. Adhere a button to the image with craft glue and allow it to dry.

## 3. Fill cap with Liquid Laminate

Fill the inside of the bottle cap with Liquid Laminate, just covering the image with a thin layer.

## 4. Apply Stickles

While the Liquid Laminate dries, apply turquoise Stickles around the profile of your image. Also apply stardust Stickles to the button. Allow the inside of the bottle cap to dry completely.

## 5. Adhere pin back

If desired, attach a pin back to the center back of the bottle cap using Amazing Goop. Allow it to dry.

## 6. Thread jump ring through top hole

To embellish the pin as shown, thread a large jump ring through the top hole in the bottle cap. Create coiled dangles with crystals and slide them all onto a small jump ring. Link the small jump ring to the bottom of the bottle cap with a large jump ring. (See Techniques, pages 15–17, for instructions on opening and closing a jump ring and for instructions on making dangles.)

## Gallery

### Sew Buttons Variation

Here's another version in black and white. I used stardust Stickles and a faceted crystal round from Beadtrust, a hammered sterling link and four jet AB CRYSTALLIZED – Swarovski Elements rounds.

## tip

*What if you use a different frame? How about a totally different style of image? You can change this up endlessly, and it's quick and easy to do.*

# iMagic

## Materials

image for manipulation*

pewter frame (HHH Enterprises)

metal charms or other collage bits
(Sacred Kitsch Studio)

22-gauge silver-plated head pins

6mm jump ring

white craft glue (Beacon)

Diamond Glaze (JudiKins)

various beads for accents

**Tools:** computer, scanner, ink-jet printer,
photo-editing software (I used Adobe
Photoshop), publishing software (I used
Microsoft Publisher), scissors, round-nose
pliers, chain-nose pliers, wire cutters,
rubber gloves

* If you intend to sell your finished piece,
always use permission-free images or scan
and alter items from your own personal
ephemera collection. Be mindful of the
potential for lawsuits if you use images that
are not yet in the public domain.

sing modern technology to manipulate vintage images just tickles me pink—it's the ultimate combination
of new and old. In the following steps, I give you the basics of digital manipulation, but you can explore the
software you have at home to create even more cool effects. I chose to feature Jean Harlow, one of the original
bad-girl blondes, but you can use any image you like here. To incorporate this pendant into a necklace, I've added
Swarovski gunmetal jet channel chain to give this design vintage appeal.

# Creating a Pendant with a Digitally Altered Image

## Gallery

### Putting on the Ritz

The background here is from a Die Cuts with a View Glitter Stack scrapbook paper collection and the foreground is a scan from an old tire ad. Look at images you find in print with digital eyes—think about what you can do with them once they're scanned into your computer. I combined the pendant with frosted vintage Lucite beads, vintage Czech glass striated squares and stunning hammered sterling chain from Bead Trust.

### 1. Alter image and print out

Select an image to use in your project—something bold and striking works best since it will be sized much smaller for jewelry. Scan the image and save it to your computer. Drag the image into your photo-editing software. (I used Adobe Photoshop 7.0.) Size the image to fit the frame. The frame I used was 2¼" × 1¾" (6cm × 4cm). Use various filters and effects to create a look you like. For example, to get the look as pictured, solarize the image by setting the brightness/contrast level to 25%. You can also apply a diffused glow and use the graphic pencil with a color saturation of -77 hue, -40 saturation and +4 lightness. Print out your finished image on good photo paper using an ink-jet printer.

### 2. Adhere image to frame

Cut out the manipulated image to fit the frame you're using. Adhere the image to the frame with white craft glue.

### 3. Adhere star charm to image

Use white craft glue to adhere a star charm on top of the image.

### 4. Apply glossy glaze

Squeeze a glossy glaze such as Diamond Glaze into the frame, completely covering the image and taking care to avoid bubbles. Allow it to dry overnight.

### 5. Create dangles

Create dangles by sliding beads onto head pins and creating a wrapped loop above each bead. (See Techniques, page 17, for instructions on making a wrapped loop.) Slide all the dangles onto a jump ring and link the ring to the top loop on the pendant. (See Techniques, page 15, for instructions on opening and closing a jump ring.)

# Lettres D'Amour

This little chipboard slide mailer makes the perfect miniature book/pendant. Just drill a hole in the back and add a jump ring after stamping, inking, découpaging and sealing the little chipboard piece, and you can wear a story around your neck. I've told a tale of young love here, *en français*. I'm off to Paris soon and it seemed fitting. It's easy to scan and print out vintage ephemera or other images you may wish to découpage so you can keep the originals intact. I kept this design simple by hanging the pendant from a long length of copper chain.

## Creating a Mini Book/Pendant Collage

## Materials

chipboard slide mailer (1½" × 3¾" [4cm × 10cm]) (ARTchix Studio)

scanned images for collage (I used vintage German paper cutouts from ARTchix Studio)

metal accents or other collage bits (ARTchix Studio)

printout of words in 14-point French script (Lettres D'Amour, Je t'adore..., toujours)

Distress Ink pads in Tattered Rose, Fired Brick and Spicy Marmalade (Ranger)

copper leafing pen (Krylon)

jet black archival ink (Ranger)

découpage medium (Mod Podge by Plaid)

Liquid Laminate (Beacon)

hot glue

black ribbon with edging for spine trim (optional)

flat-back jet CRYSTALLIZED – Swarovski Elements crystals

8mm jump ring

3-in-1 craft glue (Beacon)

dimensional foam dot stickers

French writing stamp (Hero Arts)

Liquid Pearls embossing powder in Pearl (Ranger)

**Tools:** hole punch, heat tool, hot glue gun, non-stick craft sheet, printer, computer with publishing program

### 1. Apply ink to mailer
Pounce ink onto the edges of the mailer, working with 1 color at a time. Apply the ink lightly so the board doesn't get too wet. Keep alternating colors and blending toward the center until you are pleased with the effect. Less is more here. Allow the inks to dry. (Use a heat tool to speed the process, if desired.)

### 2. Stamp text onto mailer
Ink a stamp with archival ink and stamp upside down on the top half of each foldout section and right-side up on the bottom half of each foldout section.

### 3. Adhere text and images

Adhere an image to the front and back pages of the mailer with découpage medium. Allow them to dry. Adhere words to the front and inside left pages with découpage medium. Allow them to dry.

### 4. Seal images with Liquid Laminate

Coat the chipboard with a thin layer of Liquid Laminate. Use a heat tool to dry the laminate. It will get a rough texture—this is okay.

### 5. Add copper accents

Edge the images, the inner frame and the words with a copper leafing pen. Use a heat tool to heat the edging, causing the copper leafing to bubble up, creating a rough texture. Don't heat too much!

### 6. Adhere raised image to inside of mailer

Use foam dimensional dots to adhere the cutout image of a little girl inside the inner frame.

*How many stories might you tell with this little slide mailer? You have four pages and endless variations! Try other ink colors, different texture stamps, varied images and text. Just take care not to oversaturate the paper, and you'll be golden!*

## 7. Adhere hand charm to back of mailer

Adhere a metal hand to the back of the frame over the bird image with 3-in-1 craft glue.

## 8. Adhere crystal accents

Adhere flat-back crystals to various parts of the frame using 3-in-1 craft glue.

## 9. Adhere ribbon to spine

Use a hot glue gun and glue to adhere a ribbon to the spine of your mini book.

## 10. Punch hole in top of book

Punch a hole at the top inside of the inner frame to accommodate a jump ring. Thread a jump ring through the hole. (See Techniques, page 15, for instructions on opening and closing a jump ring.)

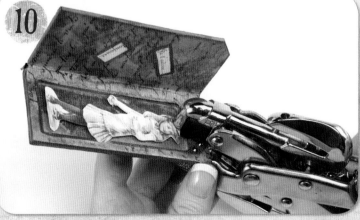

# Ephemerally Yours

## Techniques for Incorporating Ephemera

*I* have been scouring thrift shops, flea markets and antique malls for more than twenty-five years, and I've been collecting vintage magazines and old photos for about twenty years. I can sit and stare at old advertisements and greeting cards and photo albums for hours on end. *Ephemera* is the term used for fragile and fleeting vintage items, such as paper and cardboard. Ticket stubs, photographs, calling cards, journals, books, greeting cards and postcards, magazines, signs and advertising items…ephemerals for five hundred, Alex. Whether you use the actual item, cut something out from a premade ephemera sheet or scan and manipulate a piece, it's endlessly fascinating stuff. It makes you humble to realize the detritus of your existence will eventually return to the great cosmic junkyard and maybe even become part of some future person's artwork. It also makes you realize how fragile we all are and how beautiful it is to be connected, through time, to a perfect stranger.

In *How Does Your Garden Grow?* (see page 74), an image from a delightful vintage postcard I found on a recent trip to Paris makes the perfect complement to a timeless phrase. In *Burnt Offerings* (see page 80), collaged pages from old books combined with sheet music look as if they've survived a fire. You'll also learn how to make an inked, collaged altered tin and some whimsical, layered wood beads in this chapter.

# Sweet Nothings

## Materials

candy tin (Jones Soda Co.)

lovers collage image and tiny paper collage elements (ARTchix Studio)

small metal bird charm (ARTchix Studio)

mini metal filigrees (Eastern Findings)

copper crystal CRYSTALLIZED – Swarovski Elements hot-fix crystals (SS12)

22-gauge silver-plated ColourCraft wire (Beadalon)

3 6mm copper crystal CRYSTALLIZED – Swarovski Elements rondelles

paper from vintage typing manual or other interesting newspaper-style background

"intimacies" printed in 12-pt Times New Roman

alcohol inks in Stream and Meadow (Ranger)

glossy découpage medium (Mod Podge by Plaid)

Diamond Glaze (Judikins)

jeweler's cement

**Tools:** electric hand drill with 1/8" (3mm) bit, alcohol ink applicator, hot-fix crystal applicator, round-nose pliers, 2 pairs chain-nose pliers, nylon-jaw pliers, scissors, pointed metal tool, sandpaper, mask

Slip your sweet nothings inside this deliciously romantic altered tin. A love poem, a random suggestion, a saucy sentiment…whatever floats your boat, my dear. They're your fantasies, dahling—we're just making the container! This technique shows you how to create a dimensional collage with your ephemera—you might just start looking at your "trash" a bit differently. Who knows what treasures you can create just by adding an ephemera collage? Add a simple chain to turn this altered tin into a pendant that's sure to attract attention.

# Altering a Tin by Applying Vintage Ephemera and Ink

### 1. Sand tin
Sand the finish off of the tin. Clean away the dust. Wear a mask if you're sensitive to dust, like I am.

### 2. Adhere collage to tin
Cut out the paper collage accents with sharp scissors, measuring the design to be sure it fits the tin properly. Set aside. Rip sections of paper from a vintage typing manual or other newsprint-style paper. Adhere the torn paper to the tin using découpage medium. Let the adhesive dry.

### 3. Apply ink to tin
Use the alcohol ink applicator tool to dab inks onto the tin. Apply the inks to different spots of the applicator to maintain the color separation. Allow the ink to dry.

### 4. Adhere collage elements and filigrees
Adhere the cut-out paper accents and mini-collage elements of your choice to the front of the tin with découpage medium. Adhere mini-metal filigrees to the corners of the collage with jeweler's cement. Allow the adhesive to dry.

### 5. Frame collage with crystals
Frame the collage images with Swarovski hot-fix crystals using the applicator tool. It's very hot, so be careful.

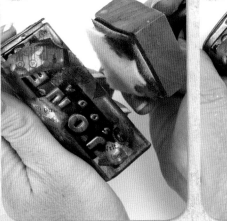

## tip

*The images and text you choose will determine the aesthetic here. What about '50s ads or '70s magazine photos? What happens if you ink the tin in psychedelic colors? How about using thin, colorful tissue paper to create a layered effect?*

## 6. Apply Diamond Glaze to tin

Squeeze a small amount of Diamond Glaze onto your finger and rub it onto the tin to seal in the remaining images and ink. Try to avoid the central image.

## 7. Apply thick coat of Diamond Glaze over collage

Squeeze Diamond Glaze onto the center collage image until you have an even, thick layer covering the collage. Avoid shaking the bottle to prevent too many bubbles from forming. Allow the medium to dry.

## 8. Drill holes in tin

Use an electric drill with a small bit to make a hole in each short side of the tin, approximately ¾" (2cm) down from the top of the tin.

## 9. Begin to create wire hanger

Cut a 4½" (11cm) piece of craft wire. Use round-nose pliers to create a small loop in 1 end of the wire. Thread the wire through a hole in the tin, pulling the wire from the inside of the tin to the outside, hiding the loop inside the tin.

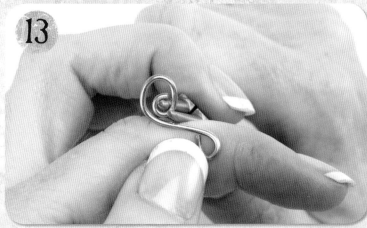

### 10. Finish wire hanger

Bend the wire flush to the top of the tin and over into a handle, inserting it into the outside of the opposite hole. Use round-nose pliers to create a second loop, bringing the wire flush to the inside of the tin.

### 11. Create bird dangle

Slide a bird charm and 3 copper crystal dangles made with ball-tipped head pins onto a 10mm jump ring. (See Techniques, page 17, for instructions on making wrapped loops.) Set the jump ring aside.

### 12. Create coiled wire accent

Cut a 2" (4cm) length of craft wire. Use round-nose pliers to start a small loop in 1 end of the wire. Begin to make a tight coil using your fingers. Clamp the coil in nylon-jaw pliers and continue coiling the wire.

### 13. Finish wire coil

Bend the free end of the wire into a loop with round-nose pliers to finish the S-shaped coil.

### 14. Finish tin pendant

Attach the coil to the handle and link the jump ring with the dangles to the handle, as well.

# How Does Your Garden Grow?

## Materials

scanned, sized and printed vintage image (or cutout image from an ephemera sheet by ARTchix Studio)

tiny printed phrase, "How does your garden grow?"

teal metal mesh tubing (Rings & Things)

2 pieces memory glass and gunmetal frame (Ranger)

Zip-Dry Paper Glue (Beacon)

10mm jump ring

22-gauge head pins

selection of beads to make dangles

**Tools:** scissors, pencil or pen for marking, round-nose pliers, chain-nose pliers, wire cutters, computer and printer (optional)

To make this mini collage, I scanned and printed a vintage postcard I found at the Paris Flea Market. I was completely enchanted by the colors and the image, and I loved the story it told. I added a metal mesh tube bow above the pendant and added bows along the chain to pull it all together. I love when designs come together organically like this one. Keep your eyes open for ephemera that would make a good framed mini collage. Colorful bead dangles tie the color scheme together and add just the right amount of swing and sparkle.

# Creating a Mini Collage Pendant with Vintage Ephemera

**1. Trace around glass onto image**
Select a vintage image you like, scan it into your computer, size it to fit the frame and print it out (or you may use the original image). Place the glass slide on top of the image and trace around it. Cut out the image to fit the slide.

**2. Manipulate mesh into shape**
Cut a small piece of mesh and stretch it out at regular intervals to create a wavy piece.

**3. Trim mesh to fit glass**
Adhere the phrase "How does your garden grow?" vertically, leaving space for the mesh. Add the wavy mesh along the right edge of the image, and trim the mesh to fit the length of the glass.

**4. Insert collage into frame**
Place another glass slide on top of the collage and mesh and slide the sandwiched collage into a frame.

**5. Make dangles**
Make several dangles with wrapped loops and slide them onto a jump ring. (See Techniques, page 17, for instructions on making a wrapped loop.) Slide the ring onto the loop at the top of the frame.

**6. Create mesh bow**
Cut a small piece of mesh and knot it in place to the loop at the top of the pendant. Stretch out the ends of the mesh to create a bow shape.

## Gallery

### The Queen Was in the Parlor

If I were Queen, you'd definitely find me "eating bread and honey." If I weren't in my studio making cool stuff, that is. Here's a mini collage in a reusable metal frame that is too cute for words. Crown me, baby! This technique is so simple you can make lots of these in no time at all.

# Numbers Game

These layered beads started out as plain wooden discs. Some black paint, a bit of numbered gaffer's tape, tiny torn words from an antique German book, a cutting of grosgrain ribbon and… a bead is born. The mixture of copper with black, red and white is a surprisingly appealing idea. I added a pretty copper clasp from Blue Moon Beads to give it a vintage touch. Using ephemera to decorate your own customized beads gives your jewelry a personal touch. To make a charm bracelet with my beads, I used a thick copper rolo chain as the base and added a pretty copper clasp from Blue Moon Beads to give it a vintage touch. The crystal beads are all from Swarovski.

## Materials

blank wooden discs (Darice)

numbered black gaffer's tape (7gypsies)

red grosgrain ribbon with stars

tiny ripped words from a vintage book

matte découpage medium (Mod Podge by Plaid)

Diamond Glaze (Judikins)

black paint dabbers (Ranger)

8mm copper jump rings

**Tools:** paintbrush, scissors, fine-grit sandpaper, mask, electric handheld drill with ⅛" (3mm) bit, pencil to mark drill holes

## Creating Beads with Wooden Discs

1

### 1. Sand and paint discs

Use fine-grit sandpaper to smooth the surface of each disc. Paint the front of each disc, and allow them all to dry. Paint the backs and sides of each disc, allowing them to dry before turning them.

## 2. Adhere first layer of gaffer's tape

Cut numbers from the gaffer's tape and adhere a numbered piece to each disc, placing the tape at an angle. Vary the placement from disc to disc. Use scissors to cut around the edge of each disc, trimming the tape so it is flush with the edge of the disc. Adhere a second layer of gaffer's tape and cut it flush to the edges of the discs as before.

## 3. Adhere collage elements to each disc

Use your fingers to carefully tear small words from the book page. Glue a word to each disc with découpage medium, varying the placement on each disc. Allow the glue to dry. Cut small stars from the ribbon and adhere them to each disc with découpage medium, using the end of a paintbrush to hold the edges of the ribbon down while you adhere it to the disc. Allow the medium to dry.

## 4. Seal collage with découpage medium

Paint the disc and collage elements with a layer of matte découpage medium. Use a finger to remove the paintbrush strokes from the medium. Allow the bead to dry.

## 5. Seal ribbon with Diamond Glaze

Put a layer of Diamond Glaze on the ribbon element. Allow it to dry. After the bead is dry, use scissors to cut off any slight overlap of gaffer's tape.

## 6. Drill holes and add jump rings

Mark the placement of drill holes with a pencil. Use the electric drill and a small bit to drill a hole through each marked spot. Thread a jump ring through each hole. (See Techniques, page 15, for instructions on opening and closing a jump ring.)

*tip*

The idea here is to layer items over a plain bead to give it dimension and visual interest. What you choose matters less than how it all works in the final composition. I'm of the less-is-more school. I suggest each time you make a collage you take one element away and see if it isn't better. If not, add it back in!

## Gallery

### Your Number Is Up

Springtime colors and some coordinating scrapbook paper combined with a different style of 7gypsies gaffer's tape work beautifully in this pretty bracelet. I'm stuck inside the old Amish schoolhouse I call home because everything is starting to come back to life and I have terrible allergies, but I love this time of year so much! I find nature a wonderful source of inspiration, and the base colors here of Mountain Rose and Lettuce Adirondack Dabbers are so springy! This cheerful design is such a contrast to the edgy black, red, white and copper look of the other piece. Never be afraid of color—it's your friend!

# Burnt Offerings

Pages from old faded books make wonderful découpage paper. To add to their overall aged appearance, I've burned them along the edges and here and there inside the wooden stars. This versatile technique can really transform your ephemera. Playing with fire has never been this much fun! The tiny keys, Swarovski crystals and delicate brass chain I used in the finished necklace design keep the focus on the stars, where it should be!

## Materials

small and large flat wooden stars (Darice)

various pages from old books in a variety of languages

matte découpage medium (Mod Podge by Plaid)

craft glue (UHU by Saunders)

Distress Ink pad in Frayed Burlap (Ranger)

**Tools:** paintbrush, foam applicator tool, wood-burning tool, handheld electric drill with a ⅛" (3mm) drill bit, pencil to mark drill holes, fine-grit sandpaper, mask, damp cloth, scissors

## Antiquing Vintage Paper with a Wood-Burning Tool

**1. Sand stars**
Sand the wooden stars with fine-grit sandpaper. Wipe away any dust with a damp cloth.

**2. Glue paper to stars**
Adhere stars to a piece of book paper with a thin layer of paper-friendly craft glue. Allow the glue to dry.

### 3. Cut around stars
Cut around each star with scissors.

### 4. Burn edges of stars
Use the wood-burning tool to burn around the edges of the stars, burning the paper and the wood.

### 5. Smooth star edges with sandpaper
Use sandpaper to gently remove any stray paper edges.

## *tip*

If you want to use new paper or chipboard instead of old paper, use a shaped tip to create more of a branded effect. Be sure to burn carefully around the edges for a consistent look. Don't burn plastic and be careful when you burn some papers because the inks may release toxins. This is a do-it-in-your-workshop and wear-a-mask task.

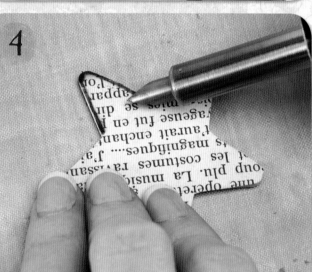

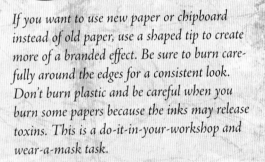

### 6. Apply ink to stars
Apply Distress Ink to one side of each star using the foam applicator tool to spread the ink. Allow the ink to dry.

### 7. Apply découpage medium to stars
Paint each star with matte découpage medium and allow them all to dry.

### 8. Mark and drill holes
If you'd like to make the stars into charms, use a pencil to mark the hole placement for each star. Drill through each marked spot with an electric drill and a small bit.

# Scrapped

## Techniques for Working with Scrapbooking Supplies

The thing about scrapbooking is that eventually your materials outpace your books. Waste not, want not! Why not repurpose those supplies for jewelry applications? It's a logical step to want to "wear your scrapbook," and it feels good to know these materials aren't going to waste away in a drawer somewhere when they could be garnering compliments from friends and family. Thanks to my dear friends Robin Beam and Rebecca Peck, I've been dragged into the inky world of paper arts. Yes, it's true, I've gone to the inky side, and I'm not coming back, people. Every scrapbook aisle item is a potential jewelry design waiting to be born; nothing—and I do mean nothing—escapes my creative grasp. Insert evil laugh here…

Crafty Genius Tim Holtz gets a gazillion kisses for developing Grungeboard, a material that combines the versatility of paper with the strength of fabric or leather. I have tried my best to ruin this stuff as I am wont to do with new things, and I simply cannot do it. *Get Your Grunge On* (see page 92) in a painted, stamped, laminated bracelet, and check out the piratey-good gallery variation! Basic chipboard circles are transformed with ink and laminate to look like ceramic discs in *I'll Fly Away* (see page 88). This chapter will inspire you to look at your leftover crafting supplies in a whole new light.

# Time Flies

## Materials

wooden flower (Provo Craft)

metal watch face (Ornamentea)

scrapbook paper (Die Cuts with a View)

"time flies" printed in 12-point Times New Roman

crackle paint (Ranger)

paint dabber (Ranger)

star stamp (Inkadinkado)

2 4mm crystal AB Swarovski flowers

2 3mm cystal AB Swarovski butterflies

1 Lucite flower (Maya Road)

1 pin back (Rings & Things)

Amazing Goop

craft glue (Beacon)

**Tools:** paint dabber, small paintbrush, sandpaper, scissors

A blank wooden flower turns funky with layers of crackle paint, stamped stars and a mini-collaged watch frame. Lightweight wood cutouts sold for use on scrapbook pages make great jewelry components. This unexpected combination of elements can change completely based on your choice of colors and finishes. I'm digging the pink and yellow combo, but maybe brown and teal is more your style. Switch it up!

# Creating a Pin with Scrapbooking Embellishments

### 1. Paint flower with basecoat
Sand the front and sides of the wooden flower. Paint the flower with a pink paint dabber. Allow it to dry. Use a small paintbrush to paint the edges of the flower pink. Allow the paint to dry. If desired, paint the back of the flower and allow it to dry.

### 2. Paint flower with crackle paint
Paint the flower with crackle paint. Allow it to dry. (Thicker paint makes thicker cracks and vice versa.)

### 3. Stamp flower
Stamp the petals with the star stamp, varying the placement of the stars from petal to petal.

### 4. Smear pink paint
Use your fingers to smear on more pink paint. Allow the paint to dry.

### 5. Adhere watch face
Adhere the watch bottom to the center of the flower with Amazing Goop. Allow it to dry.

### 6. Create collage
Cut a piece of scrapbook paper to fit inside the bottom of the watch face. Cut out the "time flies" phrase and adhere it to the scrapbook paper with craft glue. Add a selection of beads on top of the collage. Slide the watch face onto the bottom. If you want to make this a pendant, just drill a hole and add a jump ring. To make a pin, glue a pin back to the center back of the flower using Amazing Goop. Allow it to dry.

## tip

*What if you used a different shape here? How about something with dimension and texture? What if you used a smaller flower or a star and a tiny watch frame? What happens if you make it look vintage using sepia tones and old paper? Try different approaches and see what they bring to the project.*

# I'll Fly Away

To create these enamel look-alikes, I've accented Victorian-style bird-and-nest stamped images with soft shades of blue and green ink coated with glaze. Can you believe they're paper products? Chipboard provides a litany of design possibilities for the jewelry artist. Just don't wear these beads in the swimming pool, and you'll be fine. I combined my beads with gunmetal chain and findings from Rings n' Things. The darker gunmetal color gives these components a nice depth and makes the crystals sparkle in a more subtle fashion.

## Creating Faux Enameled Jewelry

## Materials

3 chipboard circles

bird-and-nest stamp set (Cavallini & Co.)

jet black archival ink (Ranger)

Distress Ink pads in Shabby Shutters and Broken China (Ranger)

Diamond Glaze (JudiKins)

Cut-and-Dry stamp foam squares (Ranger)

fine-tip black permanent marker

4mm gunmetal jump rings (Rings & Things)

gunmetal head pins (Rings & Things)

4mm olivine CRYSTALLIZED – Swarovski Elements rounds

4mm jet hemtatite CRYSTALLIZED – Swarovski Elements rounds

4mm indicolite CRYSTALLIZED – Swarovski Elements bicones

**Tools:** round-nose pliers, 2 pair chain-nose pliers, wire nippers, hole punch

### 1. Punch holes
Punch a hole in each chipboard circle.

## tip

You can do so many things with chipboard. The key is not to oversaturate it with inks. It took me a few tries to get this one right. If you want to layer inks, let them dry between each application so the paper won't warp.

## 2. Apply ink to circles

Apply Distress Ink to the front and back of each of the circles with a foam square. Use a different part of the foam for each color to prevent muddy results. Allow the ink to dry.

## 3. Stamp image onto circles

Stamp the image or images you selected onto the circles. Allow the ink to dry.

## 4. Coat circles with Diamond Glaze

Add a layer of Diamond Glaze, taking care not to shake the tube to prevent bubbles. Allow the protective coating to dry. Repeat for the back side of the chipboard.

## 5. Add black accents

Color the edges of each circle by lightly dragging a fine-tip permanent marker around the edge of each chipboard circle. Insert the tip of the permanent marker into the punched hole from the back of the piece to accent the inside of the hole with black.

## 6. Create wire loop

Thread a 4mm olivine round onto a head pin and thread the beaded head pin into the hole in the front of the chipboard circle. Bend the head pin flush to the back of the bead and create a loop.

## 7. Add dangles

Slide each bead onto a head pin and make a wrapped loop above each bead. (See Techniques, page 17, for instructions on making a wrapped loop.) Slide all of the dangles onto a jump ring. Slide the beaded jump ring onto the bail at the top of your disc and secure it closed with pliers. (See Techniques, page 15, for instructions on opening and closing a jump ring.)

**6**

**7**

# Gallery

### Enameled Flower

A Bazzill Basics chipboard pop art flower goes understated here. I inked it with layers of Distress Ink in Mustard Seed and Scattered Straw. Then I stamped it with archival ink and edged it and accented it with brushed Corduroy Distress Ink. The pendant is strung on a beaded strand featuring free-form freshwater pearls, 4mm lime, smoky quartz and jet AB Swarovski crystals, hematite beads and one large Hill Tribe silver shell bead.

### Enameled Bird Pin

I used Maya Road chipboard birds and branches to make this sweet little pin. The bird is inked with Ranger inks, including Rose Madder and Cerulean Azure mixed with Mustard Seed Distress Ink. I love how it looks almost plaid, an effect I created by applying the ink straight from the pads without any further stamping. The branch is inked with Distress Ink in various shades of brown and tan. I added a textured stamp layer in coffee archival ink. This technique can look completely different depending on how many layers you create and the colors you choose. I love the bold simplicity of this design.

# Get Your Grunge On

As soon as I saw Grungeboard I knew I could use it to make excellent jewelry components. It's flexible, durable and great for layering on inks and paints to your heart's content. Thank you, Tim Holtz! In this case, I've used layers of crackle paints, inks and rubber stamps with some metal accents to make a funky focal component. I linked the Grungeboard component to two lengths of textured brass chain to make a chunky bracelet, and I added frayed waxed linen accents as an afterthought.

## Painting, Distressing and Embellishing Grungeboard

## Materials

Grungeboard elements (Tim Holtz)

Distress crackle paint in tonally similar colors (Ranger)

Distress Ink in Vintage Photo (Ranger)

Stickles in tonally similar colors to crackle paint (Ranger)

alcohol ink in a tonally similar color, plus a metallic shade (Adirondack by Ranger)

jet black archival ink (Ranger)

Glossy Accents (Ranger)

various textured background stamps

grommets

small metal charms or accents

hot-fix CRYSTALLIZED – Swarovski Elements crystals

craft glue

**Tools:** heat tool (optional), blending tool with rubber foam, hot-fix applicator tool, ink applicator tool with felt, grommet-setting tool

## 1. Apply crackle paint to Grungeboard elements

Select and remove the Grungeboard elements you wish to use. Cover each element with a different color of crackle paint. Allow the paint to air dry or speed up the process with a heat tool.

## 2. Apply Distress Ink

Apply Distress Ink in Vintage Photo to the Grungeboard elements with the blending tool, rubbing it into the crackle paint and edging the element. Apply ink to the backs of the elements. Allow the ink to dry.

### 3. Stamp elements

Stamp each element with a different background stamp using jet black archival ink. Allow the ink to dry.

### 4. Add more ink

Add a tonally similar alcohol ink to the Grungeboard elements using your ink applicator tool and felt. Add a metallic shade of alcohol ink to the pieces with the applicator tool and felt to create a metallic sheen.

### 5. Add Stickles

Add a tiny bit of tonally similar Stickles to 1 of the elements for sparkle. Or you may opt to omit this step.

### 6. Adhere metal charms

Attach metal charms or tiny metal items to the top layer of Grungeboard with heavy-duty, metal-friendly craft glue. Allow the glue to dry.

*tip*

*You can opt to keep the paint unsealed and just use a matte finish paint, or give it some sheen with a laminate. I like both effects for different reasons. You can use strips of Grungeboard with snaps to make bracelets, adding some layered elements and finishes. It's one of those toys you simply cannot resist!*

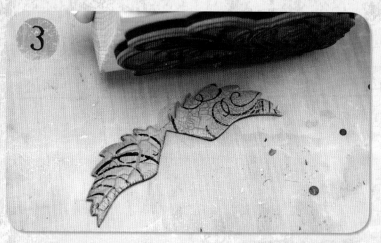

### 7. Adhere elements together
Glue the elements together to form a layered component.

### 8. Apply Glossy Accents
If you'd like a glossy finish, spread a thin layer of Glossy Accents over the surface to create a sheen.

### 9. Add hot-fix crystals
Use a hot-fix applicator tool to add hot-fix crystal accents to the bottom piece and to the wings.

### 10. Add grommets
Use a crop-a-dile or a grommet-setting tool to add grommets to the bottom piece, or where desired.

# Gallery

### Winged Heart

This pin is layered with Distress crackle paint in shades of Broken China, Mustard Seed and Worn Lipstick. Each layer is stamped with archival ink in jet black using different Hero Arts writing stamps. I added Stickles in Stardust for some sparkle, and then I adhered the layers and the pin back together with Beacon 3-in-1 glue. Ya gotta love how all three projects shown for this technique have such a different vibe using the same techniques!

### Grunge Skull

For this pirate-themed piece, I layered the skull with white crackle paint and Distress Ink in Vintage Photo. Then I stamped it with black archival ink and edged the skull in black permanent marker. The heart is layered with black crackle paint and Red Pepper dabber. The star is layered with Red Pepper dabber and stamped black archival ink. I glued it all together with Weldbond and added a grommet. Slap this on and get ready to swab the deck or shiver the timbers!

# Mud Pies

## Techniques for Working with Clay

I have loved clay since I was knee-high to a grasshopper. Many a summer afternoon in my childhood was spent making ornately embellished mud pies and three-dimensional clay sculptures. Now that I'm all grown up, I find polymer clay a very interesting medium. It has the unique ability to mimic a wide variety of other materials with a minimal amount of manipulation. The clay projects here are very rudimentary, but you can dive in deep and make canes and sculptural pieces if that's where your spirit leads you. Paper clay is another favorite of mine, mostly because it's extremely lightweight, like plastic. You can mold it and shape it into larger objects and keep adding them to your designs, if you're so inclined. It's easy to coat, color and ink in layers to make things look very old and distressed. There are many, many other kinds of clay, and each has its own charms. Get ready to roll up your sleeves and feel the squish of the clay between your fingers—we're heading back to those lazy summer days of yore.

In this chapter, you'll learn to make a mold with vintage metal components for casting paper clay. Add some metallic finish and distressing, and you've got a very cool connector in *Light as a Feather* (see page 108). You'll also discover how to combine polymer clay, rubber stamps and a fine dusting of Perfect Pearls to make realistic-looking faux metal clay links in *Forged* (see page 102). The possibilities are truly endless with this medium.

# Something Blue

These funky little beads almost didn't make it into the book. But my daughter loved them so much, I acquiesced. This is my experiment in making clay look like gemstone material and then layering the faux stones on pieces of clay in different colors, textures and shapes. I even added gold flakes to the clay to create sparkle. Consider this the seed of an idea and take it to new horizons, grasshopper. This funky pendant needed no further embellishment, so I suspended it from a delicate gunmetal chain and called it a day.

## Creating Faux Gemstones with Polymer Clay

## Materials

black, silver and blue polymer clay (Premo! Sculpey by Polyform Products)

textured stamp

gold flakes for papermaking (Arnold Grummer)

archival ink (Ranger)

5mm x 2.5mm crystal AB Swarovski flat-back rectangles

jet hematite Swarovski flat-back round

Glossy Accents (Ranger)

3 gunmetal eye pins (Rings & Things)

Shapelets plastic templates (Sculpey)

**Tools:** clay-dedicated pasta machine, clay-dedicated toaster oven, pointed clay tool, round-nose pliers, chain-nose pliers, craft knife

### 1. Condition clay
Warm the blue clay in your hands to begin to condition it. Run the clay through a pasta machine to create a thin, even sheet. (See Techniques, page 19, for instructions on conditioning clay.)

### 2. Add gold flakes to clay
Add gold papermaking flakes to the blue clay and continue running it through the pasta machine until the flakes are integrated. Don't over-condition the clay at this stage or your flakes will get lost, and you'll have to keep adding more.

### 3. Stamp clay

Ink a textured stamp with archival ink and stamp the design onto the clay using very light pressure. Don't press too hard; you don't want indent the clay.

### 4. Cut shapes from clay

Condition silver and black clay without adding flakes. Use Shapelets to create the graduated shapes from the blue clay. Lay the shapes on a sheet of black clay rolled to approximately 1/16" (2mm) thick. Cut the black clay to frame each blue shape.

### 5. Cut silver clay

Lay the stacked shapes on a sheet of silver-colored clay that is also approximately 1/16" (2mm) thick. Cut the silver-colored clay to create a 1/16" (2mm) border around the layer of black clay.

### 6. Create fluted edges

Use a pointed clay tool to create fluted edges on the silver layer of clay.

*tip*

You could make larger discs with crimped edges to look like suns or add an image transfer to the center. Try a different stamp or another combination of colors. See what other mix-ins you can add to the clay to make different effects. Seal it with a matte finish or a crackle glaze.

**7**

**8**

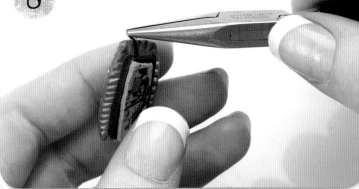

**9**

**10**

## 7. Embed crystals into clay

Use your fingers to place crystals on the clay pieces. Embed each crystal into the clay with a craft knife. Don't press too hard or you'll overbend the clay, and the stones will fall out later

## 8. Add eye pin to largest shape

Cut an eye pin to ½" (1cm) and bend the end slightly. Use chain-nose pliers to slide the pin between the silver and black clay.

## 9. Slide pins into clay squares

Separate the top layer from each of the polymer clay squares. Lay an eye pin on the bottom layer and trim the eye pin so it hangs over the square about ¼" (6mm). Turn a loop in the end of the wire. Compress the layers back together. Repeat for the second square. Bake all 3 shapes in the oven, following the manu- facturer's instructions. Allow the shapes to cool.

## 10. Coat clay with Glossy Accents

Apply a layer of Glossy Accents to each top clay piece, taking care not to get the crystals wet. Allow the gloss coat to dry. Carefully open each eye pin to connect the components.

# Forged

## Materials

black and metallic silver-colored clay (Premo! Sculpey by Polyform Products)

5 crystal AB CRYSTALLIZED – Swarovski Elements flat-back crystals

8 jet hematite CRYSTALLIZED – Swarovski Elements flat-back crystals

Perfect Pearls pigment powder in Pewter (Ranger)

unmounted textured polymer clay stamps (Sculpey)

5mm silver-plated jump rings (Beadalon)

**Tools:** clay-dedicated pasta maker, clay-dedicated toaster oven, oven thermometer, beveled geometric-edge cutters (AMACO), brushes for applying Perfect Pearls (Ranger Perfect Pearls kit), craft knife, pointed clay tool, chain-nose pliers, rubber gloves to prevent fingerprints, ceramic tile

These metallic links are definitely deceptive. Are they forged of metal or are they made of clay? Only you need know for sure, forgeress. The simple addition of a bit of metallic pigment powder turns metallic clay into a dead ringer for actual metal. Clay and rubber stamps make for hours of fun. Pick stamps designed for clay or select stamps with simple graphic images. Too much tiny detail won't indent in the clay as well. The clay discs are easy to link together with jump rings. I added a few judicious crystal accents to bring the look together perfectly.

# Creating Faux Metal Links with Metallic-Colored Polymer Clay

## 1. Cut out clay shapes
Roll silver and black clay through a pasta maker to condition it. Continue rolling the clay through the pasta maker until it is approximately ¼" (6mm) thick. (See Techniques, page 19, for instructions on conditioning polymer clay.) Cut out 4 silver circles and 4 black ovals, approximately ½" (1cm) in diameter. When working with clay shapes, you may want to wear rubber gloves to prevent leaving fingerprints.

## 2. Stamp clay
Gently press an unmounted stamp into each shape, creating a swirly imprint. Don't press too hard, or you'll go through the clay. Don't press too lightly, or the images won't be strong enough. Press like Goldilocks.

## 3. Apply pigment powder to clay shapes
Use a paintbrush to apply Perfect Pearls pigment powder to each clay shape, creating a metallic sheen on the clay surface. Make sure to thoroughly work the pigment into the clay so it adheres to the surface.

## 4. Embed crystals into clay
Place crystals in the desired locations on each bead. Press the crystals with an awl or the tip of a craft knife, gently embedding them into the clay.

## 5. Create holes in clay beads
Use the pointed clay tool to make a hole in each end of each clay bead. Make sure the holes are large enough to accommodate a standard-width jump ring. Preheat your oven to the temperature given in the manufacturer's instructions. Use a thermometer to check the temperature before baking your beads. Place the beads in the oven on a ceramic tile. Bake the clay for the recommended time. Remove the beads from the tray and allow them to cool.

## 6. Link beads
Link the beads together with jump rings and add a clasp with decorative dangles, as desired. (See Techniques, page 15, for instructions on opening and closing a jump ring.) If you like, use two matching links and some crystals to make a coordinated pair of earrings.

# Skull and Bones

A vast and ahoy, me hearties! Let's play with clay. I find myself obsessed these days with collecting and making skull and bone beads. It started with making more than fifty clay bones for a project I did for Swarovski. This pirate skull is a variation on my Day of the Dead project from my second book, *The Impatient Beader Gets Inspired!* Shaping and molding clay really is a simple, versatile technique. Don't be intimidated—just think of the clay as play dough. I dangled my skull and bone beads from a length of silver chain along with dangles made of sterling silver wave connectors, red and clear moon Swarovksi crystals, dice and eight ball beads, and key and anchor charms. A crown, a key and a moon dangle swing from the end of the extension chain.

## Materials

black and white clay (Premo! Sculpey by Polyform Products)

alcohol ink in Mushroom (Ranger)

alcohol ink blending solution, optional (Ranger)

1 8mm x 6mm jet CRYSTALLIZED – Swarovski Elements flat-back oval

3–4 crystal AB CRYSTALLIZED – Swarovski Elements flat-back rounds per bone

sterling silver eye pins (Beadalon)

sparkly découpage medium (Mod Podge Sparkle by Plaid)

**Tools:** clay-dedicated pasta machine, clay-dedicated toaster oven, pointed clay tool, chain-nose pliers, flush cutters, rubber gloves, ceramic tile

## Shaping Polymer Clay Into Three-Dimensional Forms

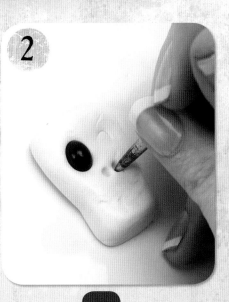

### 1. Create skull
Warm the white clay in your hands to begin to condition it. Run the clay through a pasta machine to condition it further, if necessary. Mold the clay into a small skull as shown, with a wider forehead area tapering into a narrower jaw. (See Techniques, page 19, for instructions on conditioning polymer clay.)

### 2. Make eye and nose
Press a small oval cabochon into the skull to create an eye. Use the sharp end of a pointed clay tool to make nose holes.

### 3. Create mouth

Use your fingers to roll a small piece of black clay into a thin snake. Cut the snake into 1¾" (2cm) section and 3½" (1cm) segments. Lay the longer clay segment horizontally on the skull where the mouth would be. Apply the remaining clay segments vertically over the initial segment. Gently press the clay into the skull to adhere it to the base.

### 4. Add eye patch

Flatten a small circle of black clay into an eye patch. Drape the remaining clay snake from step 3 from the upper edge of the skull above the cabochon eye to diagonally below the right eye socket, securing it by wrapping it around the side of the skull. Compress the clay to adhere it to the skull. Add the eye patch, compressing it gently to adhere it to the clay base.

### 5. Make bones

To create the bones, use a small amount of white clay and hand form it in your fingers. These look more like real bones than cartoon bones, but you can opt for a more cartoonish, stylized look if you prefer. Make as many bones as you'd like to use in your project. The pictured necklace uses 4 bones.

### 6. Add crystals to bones

Use a pointed clay tool to set flat-back crystals into the clay bones.

*tip*

*If you like, you can add crystals in different colors and sizes to the bones or leave them out all together. If you want to make a bone that looks like something you dug up, use your fingertip to apply layers of brown ink. Seal it with découpage medium.*

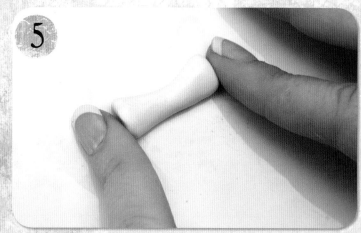

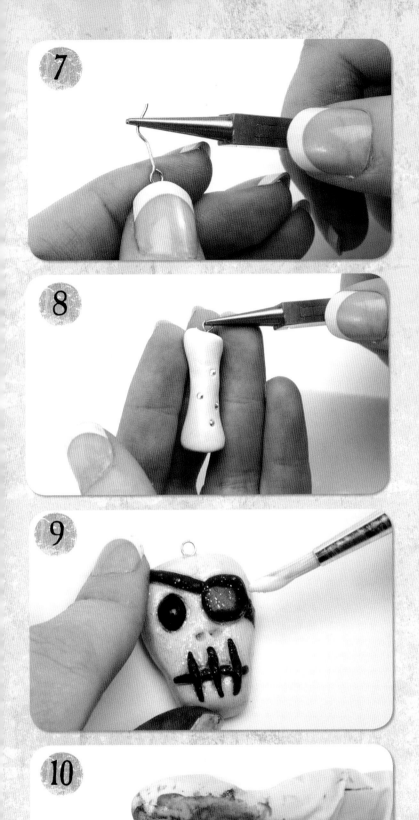

## 7. Bend eye pins for bones
Cut an eye pin to approximately ½" (1cm). Bend the ends slightly so they are not perfectly straight. Cut and bend an eye pin for each bone you made.

## 8. Insert eye pins into bones
Use chain-nose pliers to insert an eye pin into each bone, carefully sliding them in at an angle and straightening them out as you slide them in. This will keep them from easily sliding out later. Bake the clay according to the manufacturer's directions. Allow the clay to cool.

## 9. Seal skull with sparkly découpage medium
Paint the skull with sparkly découpage medium. Leave the bones unfinished for a more realistic look.

## 10. Apply alcohol ink to bones
If you'd prefer an aged look for your bones, apply layers of alcohol ink to the baked bones with your gloved fingertips. Allow the ink to dry.

## 11. Apply blending solution
Apply the alcohol ink blending solution to the inked bones and allow it to dry. (The blending solution helps even out the ink layered on the bones.) Seal the inked bones by painting on a thin layer of découpage medium. Allow the bones to dry.

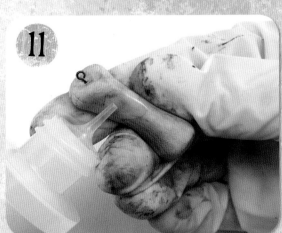

# Light as a Feather

When I found the vintage metal jewelry component I used to mold this pendant, I was instantly intrigued. By placing the clay inside the recessed back, I got a relief impression of the original component. The clay I used is made of paper, so this pendant is truly as light as a feather. I used vintage brass connectors, gold-plated chain and ornate Swarovski filigrees to create this striking necklace.

## Materials

metal component to use for mold

paper clay (Makin's Clay)

Perfect Pearls pigment powder (Ranger)

Distress Ink in Vintage Photo (Ranger)

découpage medium

water

gold chain

gold filigree components

gold clasp

jump rings

**Tools:** watercolor brush, pointed clay tool, scissors or craft knife, 2 pairs chain-nosed pliers

## Molding Paper Clay Into a Pendant

### 1. Prepare clay for mold
Knead thte paper clay briefly in your hands. This hollow vintage component allowed me to simply press the clay into the hollow back. (You can also make a mold and press the clay inside of it for a similar effect.)

### 2. Fill mold with clay
Press the clay directly into the hollow back of the item or into your mold. Smooth the back of the clay with your fingers. Let the clay harden for 10 minutes.

### 3. Remove clay from mold

Remove the clay from the mold. Use sharp scissors or a craft knife to cut away any excess clay at the edges of the component. Smooth the edges with your fingers.

### 4. Poke holes in clay

Use a pointed clay tool to punch a hole in each point of the clay piece. Allow the clay to dry overnight.

### 5. Paint clay with pigment powder

Use a watercolor brush or a damp paintbrush to paint the pigment powder onto the clay shape. You can also opt to use paints or inks or anything else to color the clay. You can also knead inks into the clay before molding. I wanted a faux enamel look, so I used a metallic pigment powder. Allow the color to dry.

### 6. Apply ink

Use your finger to rub some Distress Ink in Vintage Photo onto the clay piece.

### 7. Seal clay with protective coating

Seal the project with découpage medium or any other sealant of your choice.

### 8. Create central pendant

Link your paper clay component to beads and findings of your choice.

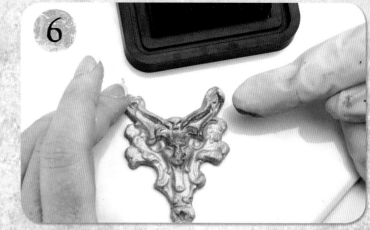

# Gallery

### Art Nouveau Necklace

A vintage glass art nouveau pendant connector made the perfect mold for a light-as-air paper clay design. I love these soft, sweet colors—they're very much out of my design comfort zone, so all the better.

# Mrs. Fix It

### Techniques for Working with Metal

Any designer worth her salt has probably discovered the joys of the hardware store. The next time you go, make sure to look with a designer's eyes. It's a virtual treasure trove of creative joy! I used to wince at the thought of a trip to the home improvement store, but now I find myself looking for excuses. Are we out of lightbulbs…again? Hey, shouldn't we fix that broken sink already? The hardware store, well, golly jeepers, I wanna go! Pick me, pick me! Not that I, independent-minded female that I am, need an excuse to go to the hardware store. It's just more fun when you can say, "Do you think I can make this into an earring?" to someone you actually know. The helpful hardware man, helpful as he is, may not have the answer to that riddle! The idea here is to jump-start your brain into looking at the ordinary things you take for granted as potential building blocks for your designs. Besides, what self-respecting crafty girl doesn't love playing with power tools?!

It's not a new idea to make washers into jewelry, but how about inking, stamping and layering them until you're not quite sure what they looked like when they started out? *All Washed Up* (see page 120) shows you how to take your everyday garden-variety washer and make it anything but ordinary. Another hardware supply, thin sheet metal, can be used in a variety of ways. In *Alchemy* (see page 118), thin glue-backed copper is inked, hammered and adhered to lightweight wooden tiles for a very interesting effect. Finally, you'll learn how to hammer metal wire on a mini anvil in *Hammered* (see page 114), a technique you can use to make all sorts of jewelry.

# Hammered

Hammering metal is actually quite a simple technique. Once you start pounding a small hammer on a tiny anvil and making hammered metal links and squiggles, all of the cares of your day-to-day world simply slip away. It's a great way to get out your aggression and make stylish jewelry parts, all at the same time. Multitasking is good. I used turquoise, khaki and indicolite Swarovski crystals on copper wire to turn these squiggles into stunning, sparkling earrings.

## Materials

20-gauge ColourCraft copper wire (Beadalon)
5mm copper jump rings (Beadalon)
clear nail polish (optional)
selection of crystals (3 for each earring)

**Tools:** mini anvil, mini chasing hammer, flush cutters, round-nose pliers, 2 pairs chain-nose pliers, sandpaper

## Hammering Metal Wire

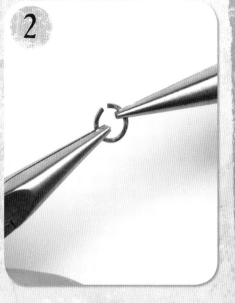

### 1. Hammer jump ring
Place a copper jump ring in the center of your anvil. It's round, and your anvil is flat. This is going to be a challenging endeavor, so prepare yourself. Hit the jump ring with the rounded end of the chasing hammer, slowly flattening and texturing the link. The link may fly away. Retrieve it if you can. You can opt to place your finger on 1 side of the link, but hit carefully to avoid hitting your precious digit!

### 2. Adjust jump ring
Reconnect the ends of the jump ring if they separate during hammering, making sure to move the ends back together laterally.

### 3. Create loop at end of copper wire

Cut 4 pieces of copper wire to varying lengths. Create a loop in an end of each wire piece using round-nose pliers. (See Techniques, page 16, for instructions on turning a loop.)

### 4. Hammer wire pieces

Slowly hammer each wire piece, flattening and texturing the wire as you work from the open end to the bottom of the loop bail.

### 5. Bend textured wire

Once the wire is sufficiently textured, use your fingers to bend it into squiggly shapes.

### 6. Sand wire end

Sand the end of the wire so it's not too scratchy.

## *tip*

*Don't stop at wire! Oh, no! Hammer metal discs and tags! Hammer until the cows come home and then hammer some more. The more you practice, the nicer it will look. In the choker shown on the next page, I used colored wire. Working with colored wire requires some finesse, or you'll nick it and expose the wire underneath. Take your time, and you'll be hammerin' like a pro in no time.*

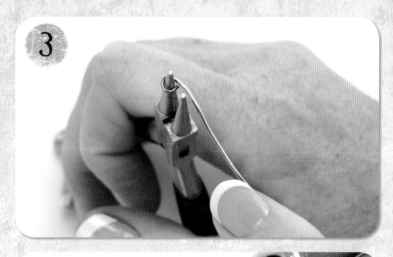

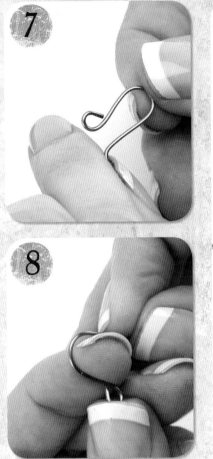

### 7. Begin to create earwires
Cut 2 2" (5cm) pieces of wire. Turn a loop in 1 end of each wire with round-nose pliers. Bend the center of the wire over your pointer finger and back over itself to make a hook. (See Techniques, page 18, for instructions on making a hook.)

### 8. Finish earwires
Use your fingers to create a slight curve in the hook near the bottom of the wire so it resembles a French earwire. Sand the ends of the wire hooks.

### 9. Link earring components
If you'd like, coat the copper findings with clear nail polish to prevent tarnishing. Allow them to dry before linking them. Link the hammered jump rings with beaded segments and slide the wavy hammered wire segments onto a jump ring at the top of the linked components. Link the earwire to this top jump ring. Repeat to make a second earring.

## Gallery

### Hammered Ring
This is a quick and easy coiled ring made with 16-gauge copper Beadalon ColourCraft wire with some hammered details on the coils. If you use copper, I suggest you seal it with clear nail polish to prevent tarnishing. I wrapped this around a mandrel to form it, and I also tried it on my own fingers while working on the design. Use nylon-jaw pliers to form the coils so you don't mar the wire. I like the primitive look of this design, but you can opt to make it more finished and use a thicker wire if you desire.

### Hammered Choker
Hammering color-coated wire is a tricky proposition; it takes a light touch and a willingness to live with a few nicks and scratches. This red necklace uses 20-gauge ColourCraft coated copper wire in red. It's suspended from memory wire inserted into a length of rubber tubing.

# Alchemy

## Materials

adhesive-backed copper sheet (Streuter Technologies)

bamboo tiles, or other predrilled flat surface (ARTchix Studio)

various alcohol inks in coordinating colors (Ranger)

texture sheets (Fiskars)

Perfect Pearls pigment powder in Copper (Ranger)

**Tools:** *chasing hammer, stylus (optional), ink applicator tool and felt, heat tool, watercolor brush, bone folder, fine-tipped permanent marker, scissors*

This super-thin sheet metal has a built-in, heat-activated adhesive. Give it a variety of finishes using alcohol inks dabbled, drizzled or dripped on the surface. It's also easy to add texture with a stylus or the rounded end of a chasing hammer. Cut the metal with scissors and adhere it to virtually anything you like using a heat tool or an iron. These beads posed a bit of a design problem because they're elongated and double drilled. To make a choker that fits snugly, you'll have to size yours to fit. After adding Swarovski jet rondelles as spacers, I made a linked extension chain to make the choker adjustable.

# Altering Copper Sheeting

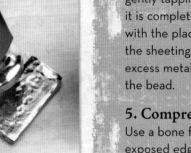

## 1. Texture metal surface

Place the copper sheet on top of a texture sheet and impress the design from the texture sheet onto the metal using the rounded end of a chasing hammer or a stylus.

## 2. Layer and blend ink

Dribble and drizzle various colors of alcohol inks onto the surface of the copper sheet. Continue layering inks, allowing them to dry and reapplying them until you're satisfied with the color variegation. Fill in any uninked places using an ink applicator tool with felt and small dabs of coordinating ink colors.

## 3. Trace shape onto metal

Trace around the bead you will be embossing with sheeting onto the metal, leaving a ¼" (6mm) edge. Cut out the shape with scissors.

## 4. Adhere metal rectangle to bead

Use a heat tool to melt the glue on the back of the sheeting to adhere it to the bead, gently tapping it with the hammer to ensure it is completely adhered. (If you are unhappy with the placement, reheat and gently shift the sheeting.) Use scissors to trim away any excess metal sheet beyond the edge of the bead.

## 5. Compress metal with bone folder

Use a bone folder to gently compress any exposed edges of the sheeting.

## 6. Apply copper pigment powder to backs and sides of beads

Use copper pigment powder and a damp watercolor brush to apply a copper color to the surfaces of the beads not covered by the sheeting.

*tip*

*This glue-backed sheeting also comes in a silver finish that looks great when embossed and colorized with dark ink. This metal sheeting will adhere to so many different surfaces—don't be afraid to play with it and see what new techniques you can discover.*

# All Washed Up

Adding inks and layers of hardware store washers to a metal blank creates a very interesting effect. The colors you select and the arrangement of the metal accents (try things other than washers for fun) will inform the finished design. If you aren't happy, you can remove the inks with an alcohol ink blending solution and reapply them. So you have full license to play freely—you can always have a do-over. I'm mad for this diamond silver-plated chain from Beadalon. It's very modern and unexpected with this metal collar.

## Materials

various sizes of metal washers

metal necklace blank (Designer Findings)

alcohol inks in Bottle, Eggplant and Lettuce (Ranger)

silver alcohol ink mixative (Ranger)

Distress powder in Faded Jeans (Ranger)

metal-friendly glue or two-part epoxy

jet black archival ink (Ranger)

small textured stamp (Japanese Stamp Set, Plaid)

clear Perfect Medium (Ranger)

acrylic paint dabber (Adirondack by Ranger)

chain

**Tools:** heat tool, ink applicator tool and felt, old toothbrush

## Inking Metal Washers and Adhering to Necklace Blank

### 1. Ink washers and necklace blank

Ink the necklace blank and the washers with 3 different colors of alcohol ink, layering the colors until you're satisfied with the results. Allow the ink to dry. For continuity, ink the back of the blank as well.

### 2. Adhere washers to necklace blank

Arrange all the washers on the blank in an arrangement you like. Glue the washers in place with a metal-friendly glue or 2-part epoxy. Allow the glue to dry overnight.

### 3. Stamp necklace

Ink a small textured stamp with archival ink and stamp it onto various spots on the necklace, alternating the orientation of the stamp to add interest.

### 4. Set ink

Use a heat tool to set the ink, keeping it moving constantly.

### 5. Spatter silver onto necklace

Dip the bristles of an old toothbrush in silver mixative and spatter silver across the surface of the metal.

### 6. Apply Perfect Medium

Dab Perfect Medium onto a few spots on the metal, working on 1 area at a time.

### 7. Apply embossing powder and heat set

Sprinkle the Distress powder onto the necklace and tap off the excess powder. Use a heat tool to set the embossing powder.

### 8. Apply ink to distressed areas

Ink the distressed areas with green or blue inks. (Avoid purple ink—it becomes too dark.) Dip your finger into some silver paint and gently dap it onto the Distress powder areas. Add a length of chain to the necklace blank to finish it.

## tip

If you opt to seal this, don't use alcohol-based acrylic spray. Why, you may ask? Well, because the alcohol will activate the inks and you'll end up with a puddle and a blank piece of metal, that's why! How do I know this? Because I did it. Duh.

7

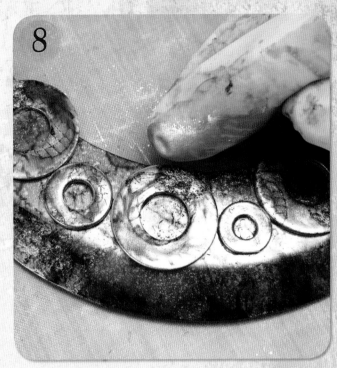

8

## Gallery

### Oversize Washer

This pendant is made entirely of metal washers with a tiny metal key accent. I applied the layers of ink before adhering things together. I let it dry overnight and then accented it all with a Japanese-themed stamp and splatters of gold metallic Ranger alcohol inks. This has a much more distressed, dark, funky vibe than the collar pendant. Make sure you use sturdy metal glue (you may want to opt for a two-part epoxy) because the washer at the top is a pendant bail. You can change this up completely by using different metals. I tried the layered ink on a copper cuff, and it looked amazing.

# Resources

The projects in this book call for a wide range of different materials. Everything you need is readily available from craft and hobby stores, hardware stores and local discount department stores. If you have trouble finding a particular product used in the book, consult the list of manufacturers below. Visit their Web sites to find out where their products are sold near you.

## Papercrafting and Scrapbooking Supplies

**7gypsies**
www.sevengypsies.com
877.7GYPSY7
*chipboard and innovative scrapbook items*

**Arnold Grummer's**
www.arnoldgrummer.com
800.453.1485
*paper-making supplies*

**Art Institute Glitter Inc.**
www.artglitter.com
877.909.0805
*ultra-fine art glitters*

**ARTchix Studio**
www.artchixstudio.com
250.478.5985
*mixed-media supplies*

**Beacon Adhesives**
www.beaconadhesives.com
914.699.3405
*adhesives and laminates*

**Cavallini & Co.**
www.cavallini.com
800.226.5287
*decorative papers and stamps*

**Die Cuts With a View**
www.diecutswithaview.com
801.224.6766
*papercrafting supplies*

**Hampton Art**
www.hamptonart.com
800.981.5169
*rubber stamps*

**Hero Arts**
www.heroarts.com
*rubber stamps*

**HHH Enterprises**
www.hhhenterprises.com
800.777.0218
*jewelry and mixed-media supplies*

**Inkadinkado**
www.inkadinkado.com
*rubber stamps*

**JudiKins**
www.judikins.com
310.515.1115
*mixed-media and paper-crafting supplies*

**Maya Road**
www.mayaroad.com
877.427.7764
*papercrafting supplies*

**Outside the Margins**
www.outsidethemargins.com
209.236.1617
*mixed-media supplies*

**Provo Craft**
www.provocraft.com
800.937.7686
*papercrafting supplies*

**Ranger**
www.rangerink.com
732.389.3535
*inks, ink applicator tools, stamp pads, UTEE, Grungeboard*

**Rubber Stampede Stamps/Delta Creative**
www.deltacreative.com
800.423.4135
*rubber stamps*

**Sacred Kitsch Studio**
www.sacredkitschstudio.com
530.680.4907
*mixed-media supplies and vintage items*

**Savvy Stamps**
www.savvystamps.com
*decorative stamps*

**Tim Holtz**
www.timholtz.com
*Grungeboard and craft supplies*

**We R Memory Keepers**
www.weronthenet.com
877.742.5937
*papercrafting supplies and tools*

## Jewelry-Making Supplies

**Beadalon**
www.beadalon.com
866.4BEADALON
*beads, wire, findings, tools*

**Bead Trust**
www.beadtrust.com
510.540.5815
*beads and jewelry supplies*

**Create Your Style
with Crystallized—
Swarovski Elements**
www.create-your-style.com
*precision-cut Swarovski crystals*

**Designer's Findings**
www.designersfindings.net
262.574.1324
*findings*

**Fusion Beads**
www.fusionbeads.com
888.781.3559
*Swarovski crystals, art beads,
jewelry supplies*

**Great Craft Works**
www.greatcraftworks.com
610.431.9790
*beads and jewelry-making supplies*

**Ornamentea**
www.ornamentea.com
919.834.6260
*jewelry-making and mixed-
media supplies*

**Phoenix Jewelry and Parts**
www.phoenixbeads.com
212.278.8688
*beads*

**The Beadin' Path**
www.beadinpath.com
877.92.BEADS
*vintage beads and jewelry supplies*

**York Novelty Imports**
www.yorkbeads.com
800.223.6676
*Czech glass beads*

## Miscellaneous Supplies

**AMACO**
www.amaco.com
800.374.1600
*pasta maker*

**Creative Paperclay**
www.paperclay.com
800.899.5952
*paper clay*

**Etchworld**
www.etchworld.com
800.872.3458
*etching cream and stencils*

**Krylon**
www.krylon.com
800.4KRYLON
*paints and pens*

**Nicole Crafts**
www.nicolecrafts.com
*craft supplies*

**Plaid**
www.plaidonline.com
800.842.4197
*craft supplies*

**Polyform Products**
www.sculpey.com
*polymer clay and supplies*

**Sharpie**
www.sharpie.com
800.323.0749
*permanent markers*

**Shrinky Dinks**
www.shrinkydinks.com
800.445.7448
*shrink plastic and supplies*

**Streuter Technologies, Inc.**
www.streuter.com
888.989.3832
*adhesive-backed metal sheeting*

**The Game Store**
www.thegamestore.com
*dominoes and game supplies*

**Walnut Hollow**
www.walnuthollow.com
800.950.5101
*craft supplies and tools*

# Index

# Check Out These North Light Books for More Inspiration and Instruction

### The Impatient Beader Gets Inspired!

*by Margot Potter*

Don't be afraid—get out there and find your inner art girl. You have terrific jewelry designs in your head just itching to get out. In a follow-up to her first beading book, jewelry designer Margot Potter gives you 40 sassy step-by-step jewelry projects plus the know-how you need to springboard off of her designs and create your own customized pieces. You'll also get regular visits from cartoon Margot, in outfits that match the theme of each chapter. Watch out for the item that inspired each piece—and don't be surprised if you get some ideas of your own.

ISBN-13: 978-1-58180-854-4
ISBN-10: 1-58180-854-2
paperback, 128 pages, Z0109

### Simply Beaded Bliss

*by Heidi Boyd*

Break away from the every-day bead-and-string combo with *Simply Beaded Bliss*. In this book, you'll learn how to incorporate mixed-media elements including paper, sequins, miniature toys and even fishing tackle into your jewelry. You'll discover how to use fingernail polish to create the look of enamel and how to link basic snaps to form the core of a charm bracelet. Choose from more than 50 simple projects that combine classic beading techniques with mixed-media elements—all with Heidi Boyd's signature Simply Beautiful style.

ISBN-13: 978-1-60061-095-0
ISBN-10: 1-60061-095-1
paperback, 144 pages, Z2004

### Bent, Bound & Stitched

*by Giuseppina Cirincione*

Collage, cards and jewelry with a twist! The author of *Collage Lost and Found* gives you 40 new techniques for incorporating unique elements into your artwork. Learn to shape wire into letters and numbers to spell out messages on cards and collages. See how stitching creates texture and brings a whole new dimension to jewelry and collage. You'll also learn to combine rivets with shrink plastic and how to rework found objects into jewelry. Best of all, each of the 20 step-by-step projects is in Josie's original style—equal parts romantic, minimalist and industrial.

ISBN-13: 978-1-60061-060-8
ISBN-10: 1-60061-060-9
paperback, 128 pages, Z1752

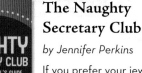

### The Naughty Secretary Club

*by Jennifer Perkins*

If you prefer your jewelry subtle and serious, this may not be the book for you. However, if kitschy accessories made with a wink and a smile are your cup of tea, this book will have you on the edge of your office chair. *The Naughty Secretary Club* is packed with more than 50 fun, secretary-themed jewelry projects, plus lots of quirky sidebars covering hot topics such as office romances and the best secretary theme songs to play on your lunch break. Jennifer Perkins, the original Naughty Secretary, will teach you how to turn almost anything into a charm, including plastic gnome cake toppers, doll furniture and cast-off hotel keys. So cancel your afternoon meetings and send yourself a memo to whip up a new paperclip necklace just in time for happy hour!

ISBN 13: 978-1-60061-116-2
ISBN 10: 1-60061-116-8
paperback, 144 pages, Z2123

These and other fine North Light books are available at your local craft retailer, bookstore or online supplier. Or visit our Web site at www.mycraftivity.com.